le corbusier
inside the machine for living

First published in the United States of America in 2000 by
The Monacelli Press, Inc.
10 East 92nd Street, New York, New York 10128

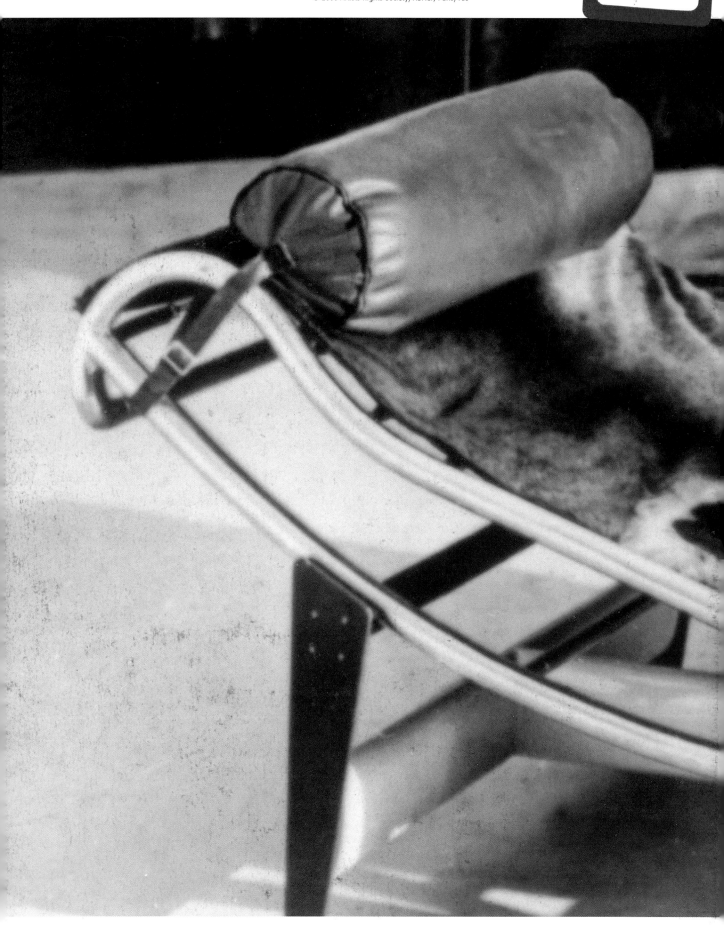

Library of Congress Catalog Card Number: 00-107362
ISBN: 1-58093-076-X

Book designed by Tracey Shiffman with Annabelle Gould.
This edition was typeset in Dax, designed by Hans Reichel, 1995–97.
Printed and bound in Italy.

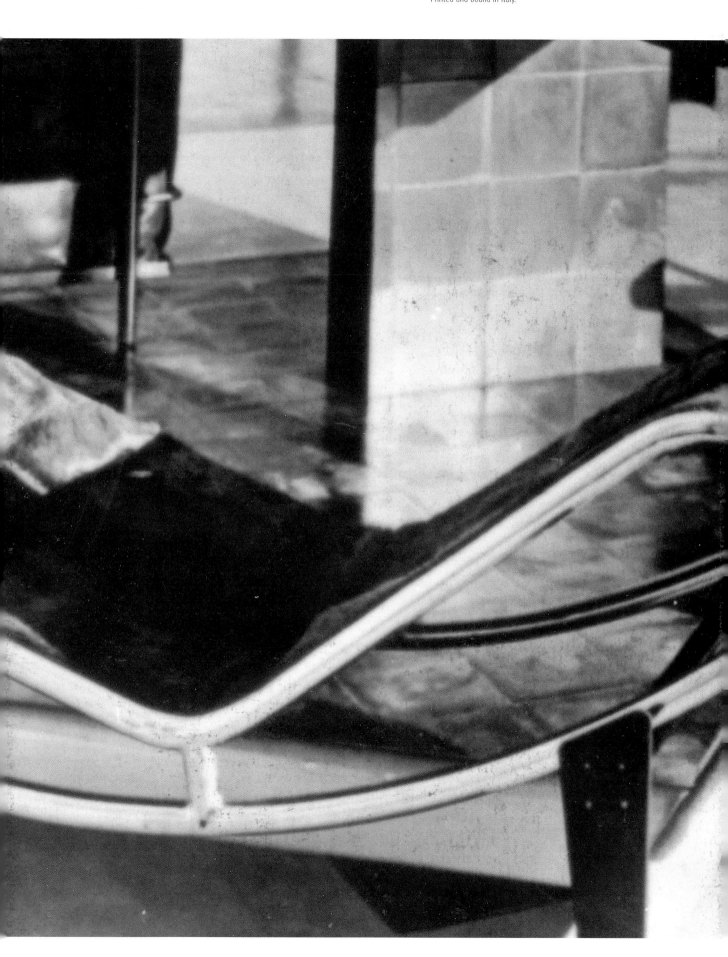

The Monacelli Press

inside **le corbusier**

the machine for **living**

george h. marcus

furniture and interiors

for david

A Style Misconstrued

introduction

Le Corbusier spoke—and wrote—too much, at least for those who might prefer to consider the work of this giant of twentieth-century architecture and design objectively, free from a rhetoric spoken in a past time and addressed to a past generation. Throughout his life, he published voluminously and lectured widely, setting down, refining, and restating his broad, redemptive ideas on the future of the city, the building, and the object. Every engagement with Le Corbusier is a balancing act. It is not enough to confront the visual and spatial immediacy of his projects; we have to evaluate them intellectually within the context of his words and his ideas. As he insisted in his book *Creation Is a Patient Search*, "certain things have to be thought out in the abstract, to be debated in the mind or aloud, alone or in friendly (or unfriendly) discussion."[1] Not that the profundity of his ideas or his writings is under question, even if his faith in their universal validity may have proven false over the years. To the contrary, his thoughts on what modern furnishings and modern houses and modern cities should be are so persuasive and so fervently described that as we read them we are pulled along with him on every detail; we take his words literally rather than metaphorically, as if, for example, his design for a city of three million inhabitants with its housing blocks marching in cadence to infinity (fig. 1) were more than a visionary, utopian construct, more than just indicative of a corrective direction he thought the future should take.

The statement that got Le Corbusier into the most trouble was his dictum "a house is a machine for living in" (and its corollary, "an armchair is a machine for sitting in"). Instantaneously it guaranteed him a place in the history of architecture, but became a cliché that has been quoted in virtually every discussion of the meaning of modern design since it was first published in 1921 in his magazine *L'Esprit Nouveau*.[2] While he clearly defined the house-chair-machine as a well-designed, well-oiled, and smooth-running organism, and reclaimed this phrase as a benchmark as he periodically reassessed his own progress in creating a new vocabulary for domestic architecture and furnishings, the statement has often been misconstrued; it was taken literally to link Le Corbusier with the imperative of a machine imagery and with the functionalist notion that form should be defined by utility. He himself repudiated such a narrow interpretation when in 1929 he asked rhetorically if we must limit architectural problems "simply and solely to the satisfaction of utility? Do poetry, beauty, and harmony enter into the life of modern men and women; or must we consider its scope as being confined to the mechanical performances of the mechanical functions postulated by 'the machine for living in'?"[3]

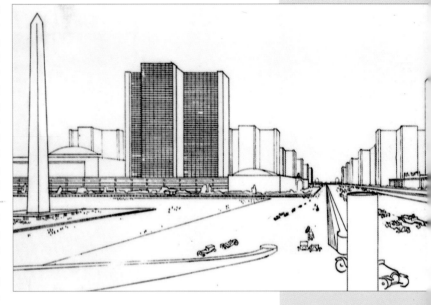

Even more so for his tubular-metal furniture (created in 1928 with his cousin and partner Pierre Jeanneret and their assistant Charlotte Perriand) than for his buildings, the idea of a machine style has compromised Le Corbusier's reputation, not by diminishing it but by confusing his work with that of other, equally inventive modernist architects and designers. Between 1925 and 1927, the Hungarian Marcel Breuer, the German Ludwig Mies van der Rohe, and the Dutchman Mart Stam all gave form to groundbreaking examples of furniture in metal. Shortly after, Le Corbusier and his colleagues worked out theirs, while a myriad of other designers were also experimenting with works in this medium. This sizable production would soon come to be perceived as a collective machine style, unified, seamless, and undifferentiated, which obscured the distinct individual and nationalistic characteristics of each of the separate works and their creators. By the 1960s, when the adherence to functionalist design was being forcefully promoted, and metal furniture from the 1920s had been reintroduced to the market, objects of this type were subsumed into what was vaguely termed the "Bauhaus style," although most of their designers, including Le Corbusier, had little or nothing to do with this seminal German design school.

Gallic rather than Germanic, Le Corbusier took a somewhat different approach from Breuer, Mies, and Stam, and his furniture must be distinguished clearly from that of the others—as well as from his own machine rhetoric. Marcel Breuer's smart, geometric armchair of 1925 was the first piece of modern-style furniture to use tubular metal for its entire structure (fig. 2). Designed when he was a teacher at

1 Contemporary City for Three Million Inhabitants, 1922. Print. Fondation Le Corbusier, Paris (29.712). **2** Marcel Breuer. Armchair, 1925. Made by Standard-Möbel. Chrome-plated steel and canvas. The Museum of Modern Art, New York. Gift of Herbert Bayer. **3** Le Corbusier, Pierre Jeanneret, and Charlotte Perriand. Armchair with pivoting back, 1928. Made by Thonet Frères. Chrome-plated steel and canvas. The Museum of Modern Art, New York. Gift of Thonet Frères.

1

the Bauhaus (although he worked on it completely independently of the school), the chair was both an exercise in the complex planar geometrics then characteristic of the institution's output and a product conceived with the mechanics of industrial manufacture and the economics of efficient distribution firmly in mind. The armchair of 1928 by Le Corbusier, Jeanneret, and Perriand (fig. 3), which superficially resembles Breuer's, had a quite different origin. It follows a vernacular model and partakes of Le Corbusier's concept of types, forms that have evolved to function well over a long period of time and that have been widely accepted for everyday use. Le Corbusier saw such antecedents as standardized solutions to basic daily needs, what he called the "tools" or "equipment" of modern life, and for the most part he was more interested in selecting such time-honored objects for his buildings than in creating new ones.

Overriding the conceptual basis of this armchair, however, is the stylish individuality of its design. Peter Blake, an architect and critic writing at the end of the 1950s when tubular-metal furniture was being reconsidered, clearly saw the distinction: "The quality that distinguished Corbu's designs from those of the Bauhaus," he wrote in *The Master Builders*, a comparative study of Le Corbusier, Mies van der Rohe, and Frank Lloyd Wright, "was exactly the same that distinguished German functionalism from Corbu's rather special brand: while Breuer's chairs were entirely rational, technically impeccable, and, incidentally, very handsome, Corbu's were neither particularly rational, nor especially easy to manufacture. All they were, in fact, was ravishingly beautiful." They were also highly eccentric, as Blake noted in describing this chair: "There are two chromium tubes that connect the front legs to the rear legs. In a Bauhaus chair these tubes would, quite obviously and soberly, have been straight. But in the Corbu chair the tubes start out straight and then, for no particular reason at all, suddenly leap up in a quarter-circle before they join the rear legs. This and other little details . . . make [Le Corbusier's] just about the wittiest, sexiest chairs designed in modern times."[4]

Beauty—not function or utility—in fact was Le Corbusier's guiding force, what he considered "the true lesson of architecture."[5] For much as this architect had gained renown for his functionalist rhetoric of utility, standardization, and the machine, above all he was a painter and a poet, steeped in his own reading of history and the premises of the traditional education he had received, ready to override theory with the aesthetics of his own design sensibility whenever it was required.[6] Born Charles-Edouard Jeanneret in 1887 in the Swiss watchmaking center of La Chaux-de-Fonds in the Jura Mountains not far from the French border, he received

2 3

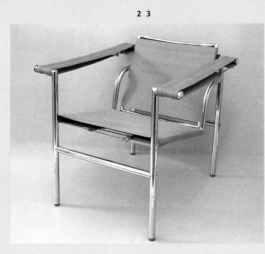

4

CHAMBRE DE LA JEUNE FILLE

this time. Together they formulated a new post-Cubist artistic movement, which they dubbed Purism, with an austere aesthetic that relied for its imagery on the simple forms of the standard, mechanically produced objects—bottles, glasses, and books—they encountered every day.

In 1920 Jeanneret opened his own architectural office, and in 1922 he was joined by his cousin Pierre Jeanneret (1896–1967). They worked together and jointly signed all the firm's buildings and architectural projects until circumstances forced them to leave Paris, and they separated, at the beginning of the Second World War. Soon Charles-Edouard Jeanneret changed his persona by adopting the pseudonym Le Corbusier (a version of a family name he had begun to use earlier to sign his architectural writings in *L'Esprit Nouveau*) and rewrote his "biography," shedding from his dossier those of his fledgling works from the past decade, mostly decorative projects and buildings done in La Chaux-de-Fonds (fig. 4), that did not fit into the modern view of architecture he had lately conceived. And in the seven volumes of his *Oeuvre complète*, the catalog of the firm's total output, published between 1929 and 1965, the year of his death, he would continue carefully to orchestrate his image, editing what would be included and the way in which it would be presented. He joined the illustrations of his works with polemical texts that informed his readers of their significance and made them aware as well of the struggles he had endured in trying to bring them to fruition, revealing an idealism and a missionary zeal that often led to bitter disappointment.[7] Although some of his complaints seem to have been exaggerated and others were the result of misunderstandings, he in fact suffered a number of major setbacks throughout his career because of the advanced strategy of his architectural ideas. Devastating above all was the loss of the most prestigious competition of the 1920s, the League of Nations building in Geneva (1927), when a committee inclined more toward conventional design took advantage of a minor technicality to strip his proposal of the first prize it had been awarded by an international committee of architects.[8]

During the 1920s Le Corbusier published influential books on architecture, decorative arts, and urbanization (the majority collected from articles that had appeared earlier in *L'Esprit Nouveau*), which were among the most widely read

little formal architectural training. What he knew came from conventional artistic studies under Charles L'Eplattenier at the school of art in La Chaux-de-Fonds; from his time as an apprentice in the architectural offices of Auguste and Gustave Perret in Paris (1908–9) and Peter Behrens in Berlin (1910–11); and from his eye-opening travels through Eastern Europe, Turkey, Greece, and Italy between 1907 and 1911, known to us through his letters and his notations and drawings in the many sketchbooks he kept. Settling in Paris in 1917 at the age of thirty, he met the extremely worldly painter-designer Amédée Ozenfant and soon began to collaborate with him, taking up his own painting seriously at

statements on the modernist movement issued during that period and built his international reputation: *Towards a New Architecture* (1923), *The City of To-Morrow and Its Planning* (1925), *The Decorative Art of Today* (1925), and the still untranslated *Almanach d'architecture moderne* (*Almanac of Modern Architecture*, 1926).[9] In these works, Le Corbusier carefully molded his image as the prototypical rationalist architect, using the houses he had recently constructed, the multiple dwelling concepts he had proposed, and the reductive interiors he had outfitted as his examples of contemporary architecture and design. With these, and subsequent, domestic projects completed throughout the decade, Le Corbusier worked out his aesthetic of modern life, but this too was misconstrued. His interiors, such as the studio he designed for Ozenfant in 1922, were understood correctly as spare, open, and full of light (fig. 5), but also incorrectly as monochromatic and coldly austere: the rich tones of their furnishings and the Purist colors with which even the most often reproduced of his houses were selectively painted were eclipsed through their publication almost solely in black and white. Just as the tubular-metal furniture was drawn into a collective machine style based on theoretical expectations, the interiors were defined by a concept of modernism, which he himself promoted, that emphasized the smooth, white walls over the colored ones.[10] In the following decades, after he had left Purist geometry behind, he continued to rely on color to animate his houses, but expanded his vocabulary to embrace a variety of building materials that also brought them a rich, textural complexity. After the war, when he startlingly changed directions, and his buildings took on a sculptural and expressive style (most notably the pilgrimage chapel at Ronchamp), he added a chromatic pageantry and a deliberate interest in surface pattern that brought decorative overtones as well as a new verve into his work.

Le Corbusier's own home and studio, the top floors of an apartment house he and Jeanneret built on the fringe of the Parisian neighborhood of Auteuil between 1931 and 1934 (fig. 6) and furnished with the help of Charlotte Perriand (1903–99), disputes particularly well the stereotype of sterility that has plagued his—and most—modernist architecture. Unlike the brilliant, unencumbered anonymous space of Ozenfant's studio, this was a complex, picturesque composition that evolved over the three decades he lived there with his wife, Yvonne, whom he married in 1930. It was an interior fully evocative of the personalities and interests of its inhabitants. It was casual and additive, mixing smooth, flat plaster walls with dramatic building vaults and found stone and brick party walls that recalled the vernacular forms of Mediterranean building, which he had discovered on his youthful travels. They established the background for the paintings he created (fig. 7), the tableaux in which he grouped the artifacts of ancient civilizations and folk cultures and the natural specimens he collected, and the modern and vernacular furnishings that made his home comfortable (fig. 8). This was an expression of his personal approach to creating an ambience for his own artistic and spiritual well-being, as he explained in 1935 when he offered his studio as the setting for an exhibition of "primitive" art in modern interiors: "The art of being able to group objects together is, in some way, an expression of modern sensitivity towards the past, towards exoticism, and towards

12 13

6 Apartment house at 24, rue Nungesser-et-Coli, Paris, 1931–34. Pencil, colored pencil, and ink. Fondation Le Corbusier, Paris (13.382). Le Corbusier's apartment and studio occupied the top two floors.   **7** Le Corbusier's apartment at 24, rue Nungesser-et-Coli. Dining room.

8 (pages 14,15) Le Corbusier's apartment at 24, rue Nungesser-et-Coli. Living room. **9** Le Corbusier's apartment at 24, rue Nungesser-et-Coli. Bedroom. The wardrobe is built onto the back of the large pivoting door. **10** Le Corbusier's apartment at 24, rue Nungesser-et-Coli. Bedroom. A rounded shower juts from the back wall, and the bed is raised high on thin tubular metal legs to take advantage of a view over the terrace parapet. **11** Plan of the first floor of Le Corbusier's apartment. Ink and pencil. Fondation Le Corbusier, Paris (13.496). The studio is to the left and the living quarters are to the right. **12** Staircase to the second floor and roof terrace of Le Corbusier's apartment. **13** Le Corbusier at home.

9 10

11

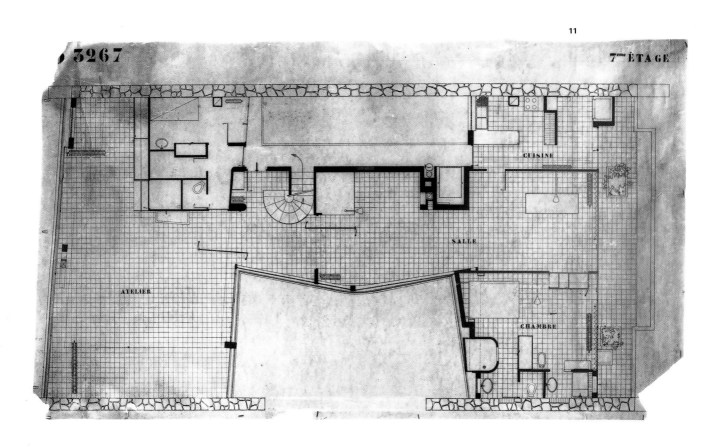

the present. It is the ability to form 'sets' or 'series,' to create 'unities' out of different periods, to once again render the element of excitement and novelty to those things which man created at some point in the past."[11]

The apartment did not rigorously follow the dictates of his geometric modernist rhetoric; it was instead a practical, multi-use interior of accommodation carefully carved out of a tight space, with irregular openings and partitions with rounded profiles, cabinets fitted out for very specific uses, light bulbs on poles jutting perpendicularly from the colored walls, a clothes storage unit slapped on the back of the oversize bedroom door (fig. 9), and a double bed raised exceptionally on tubular legs to afford a view out over the exterior parapet to the trees beyond (fig. 10). Its bipartite plan (fig. 11), as Perriand described it, reflected Le Corbusier's "theory of the couple":

12

> Monsieur and Madame separated in two spaces linked by a corridor with a meeting point in the center. This is what created the apartment's plan. At right of the entrance, to the east, was the master's studio—taboo. There he would write and paint; there his order would reign. At left, . . . to the west, was Madame's domain, comprising the kitchen, dining room, and Monsieur and Madame's bedroom (a strain to his theory). At the intersection of these two spaces: the area for receiving friends, as well as access to the upper floor [fig. 12], containing a separate bedroom and a roof garden. . . . Here Corbu received his friends—not impostors, not curiosity seekers, but those he had chosen. It was an honor.[12]

Here amid family and friends in this aerie totally imbued with his personality and his carefully chosen possessions, Le Corbusier could shed his public persona as architect and rhetorician and relax and paint as he wished (fig. 13).

NOTES

1. Le Corbusier, *Creation Is a Patient Search*, trans. James Palmes (New York: Frederick A. Praeger, 1960), 299.
2. Le Corbusier–Saugnier, "Des yeux qui ne voient pas . . . les paquebots," *L'Esprit Nouveau* 8 (1921): 848; trans. as "Eyes Which Do Not See: Liners," in Le Corbusier, *Towards a New Architecture*, trans. Frederick Etchells (London: John Rodker Publisher, 1927), 89.
3. Le Corbusier, introduction to the first edition, trans. P. Morton Shand, *Le Corbusier et Pierre Jeanneret: Oeuvre complète de 1910–1929*, ed. W. Boesiger and O. Stonorov, 4th ed. (Zurich: Les Editions d'Architecture Erlenbach, 1946), 11.
4. Peter Blake, *The Master Builders* (New York: Alfred A. Knopf, 1960), 66–67.
5. Le Corbusier, letter addressed to a group of modern architects in Johannesburg, September 23, 1936, in *Oeuvre complète de 1910–1929*, 4th ed., 6.
6. See Le Corbusier, "The Modulor: A Harmonious Measure to the Human Scale Universally Applicable to Architecture and Mechanics," in *Modulor I and II*, trans. Peter de Francia and Anna Bostock (Cambridge, Mass.: Harvard University Press, 1980), 130.
7. For the origins of Le Corbusier's idealism and his feelings of martyrdom, see Paul Venable Turner, *The Education of Le Corbusier* (New York and London: Garland Publishing, 1977).
8. The lengths to which Le Corbusier went to try to reclaim the commission are documented in *Une Maison—un palais* (Paris: Les Editions G. Crès et Cie, 1928), 195–214.
9. In the Collection de "L'Esprit Nouveau" series published by Les Editions Georges Crès et Cie, Paris.
10. The meanings of the white walls of modern architecture are extensively explored by Mark Wigley in *White Walls, Designer Dresses: The Fashioning of Modern Architecture* (Cambridge, Mass., and London: MIT Press, 1995).
11. Quoted by Jacques Sbriglio, *Apartment Block 24 N.C. and Le Corbusier's Home* (Basel, Boston, and Berlin: Birkhäuser Verlag, 1996), 57, 60.
12. Charlotte Perriand, *Une Vie de création* (Paris: Editions Odile Jacob, 1998), 55–56.

2

rhetoric

For Charles-Edouard Jeanneret, newly arrived in Paris as the First World War was ending, civilization was at a turning point. "Everything is being reorganized, clarified, purified," proclaimed *Après le Cubisme (After Cubism)*, the manifesto of Purism that he and Amédée Ozenfant published in 1918.[1] Convinced that a "new spirit" in art was ahead, they defined a new, inclusive cultural movement that demanded simplicity, permanence, harmony, and order, a reaction to the visual legerdemain that had been the signature of prewar Cubism. Purist tenets would be more fully elaborated through many of the articles and illustrations that appeared in the magazine they founded in 1920 with the poet Paul Dermée, *L'Esprit Nouveau*, which was announced as a "review of aesthetics [that] will clearly extend beyond traditional boundaries and will appropriate all the fields in which tendencies that have a considerable importance in modern life are revealed."[2] By the time the magazine ceased publication in 1925 after twenty-eight issues (and the two painters went in different directions), *L'Esprit Nouveau* had published articles about everything from painting and music to science, industry, and politics, and many were vehicles for Le Corbusier to expound his rhetoric on architecture, urbanism, and design.

In 1925, in advance of the opening of the long-awaited Exposition Internationale des Arts Décoratifs et Industriels Modernes in Paris, where the Cubistic, geometric style that would become known as Art Deco was seen at its height, Le Corbusier collected a number of his articles on the meaning of objects from *L'Esprit Nouveau* and issued them in book form as *The Decorative Art of Today*.[3] His immediate purpose was to provide a ready justification for the type of modern furnishings and interior design that visitors would see in the Esprit Nouveau pavilion that he and Pierre Jeanneret were creating for the exposition, just as his earlier compilation, *Towards a New Architecture* (1923),[4] established the justification for the pavilion as the prototype of a modern apartment dwelling unit, a repeatable building "cell." With clipped sentences, a litany of oracular repetitions, a plethora of italics, and a good dose of irony, he wove his argument, opening the first chapter of *The Decorative Art of Today* under the "sign" that had denoted articles about the upcoming exposition in *L'Esprit Nouveau* (fig. 14).

It was Le Corbusier's contention that "*modern decorative art is not decorated*," but lacking—and lamenting the lack of—a suitable alternative word to describe objects of daily use, he was left with little but the paradox of adopting the term he despised. "The paradox lies not in reality," he explained, "but in the words. Why do the objects that concern us here have to be called *decorative art*? This is the paradox:

why should chairs, bottles, baskets, shoes, which are all objects of utility, all *tools*, be called *decorative art*?"[5] The question of course was rhetorical; Le Corbusier was challenging not so much the term *decorative art* as the holdover of ornamentalism and historicism that the term evoked. He was fighting the legacy of the decorative styles that had succeeded one another in Europe over the centuries (fig. 15), which had been revived to coexist helter-skelter during the nineteenth century and continued to inspire a good deal of decoration in the twentieth. But in fighting the historic styles of the past, he was also inadvertently challenging the economic well-being of the French artistic furnishings industry centered in the Faubourg Saint-Antoine in Paris. It was the Faubourg's inexpensive, bread-and-butter reproductions and designs in various revivalist styles made for a lucrative market at home and abroad that was encouraging the proliferation of the type of decoration to which Le Corbusier was objecting. To make matters worse, as a Francophile Swiss resident in Paris, Le Corbusier was also taking a decidedly unpatriotic stance: at a time when post–World War I anti-German feeling was still strong in France (Germany was only belatedly extended an invitation to participate in the Paris exhibition in 1925, which it boycotted), he was adopting foreign attitudes that he had first encountered over a decade before on an extended study trip to Germany. There, the young architect had been most interested in the strides that had been made to bring art and industry together, to apply the creativity of the artist to the design of products for serial manufacture. He neatly documented the organizations and institutions he visited that had adopted this revolutionary approach in a small book,

14 Le Corbusier's "sign" for the upcoming Exposition Internationale des Arts Décoratifs et Industriels Modernes of 1925. From *L'Esprit Nouveau* (1924).

15 "The dictionary of the styles over the ages, and the bric-à-brac of our own times." From *L'Esprit Nouveau* (1924). **16** Peter Behrens. Kettle, 1909. Brass and cane. Philadelphia Museum of Art. Purchased with funds contributed by Gregory and Emily Harvey.

15

Etude sur le mouvement d'art décoratif en Allemagne (Study of the Decorative Arts Movement in Germany), published in 1912.[6] He espoused the principles of simplicity, the restriction of ornamentation, and the standardization of design he had seen put into practice by industry there, principles that were anathema to the French emphasis on individual craftsmanship based on the historic styles of the past.

This foreign approach to design had been especially apparent to him from the moment he arrived in Berlin in 1910, in time for the third annual congress of the Deutscher (German) Werkbund. This association of manufacturers and designers had been founded in 1907 with the goal of improving the quality of manufactured goods through the collaboration of artists and industry and of creating a national style dependent on the spirit of the new age. He had almost immediately been taken to see the factories and products of the giant general electric company, the Allgemeines Electricitäts-Gesellschaft (AEG), designed by Peter Behrens, with whom he would soon serve an apprenticeship of a few months. Behrens was the artistic director for AEG, in charge of everything from the company's electrical components and consumer products to its buildings, its graphics, and its advertising. The company had standardized many of the internal parts of its equipment to make mechanical and electrical elements interchangeable, and when Behrens, an artist by training, was hired for this job in 1907 (thereby setting an important precedent for bringing artists into German industry), he adopted a similar approach to the design of external form. He simplified such products as lighting devices and electric teakettles so that standardized parts could be used in each model regardless of its shape or finish, and he rationalized them for serial, machine manufacture, espousing a style he thought appropriate for the machine (fig.16). The young traveler noted admiringly in his journal that the forms of AEG objects had "been taken to

17
18

17 Commercial glassware and crockery. From *L'Esprit Nouveau* (1924).   **18** Charles-Edouard Jeanneret. *Composition*. From *L'Esprit Nouveau* (1924).   **19** Amédée Ozenfant. *Nacres, No. 2*, 1923–26. Oil on canvas. Philadelphia Museum of Art. Purchased with the Edith H. Bell and the Edward and Althea Budd Fund.

19

their most simple aspect . . . all the beauty lying in the proportions, and the finish of the material. These severe, ample forms are above all impressive, not pretty, they are neutral, perfectly appropriate to their use."[7]

Behrens's championship of Germanic simplicity was strongly reinforced for Le Corbusier by the Austrian architect Adolf Loos, in particular through his essay "Ornament and Crime." Although he had seen Loos's buildings in Vienna during this trip in 1910, he seems to have become aware of his writing only later, in 1913, when "Ornament and Crime" appeared in French translation in *Les Cahiers d'Aujourd'hui*. In this article (which would be reprinted in *L'Esprit Nouveau* in 1920[8]), Loos announced that the "evolution of culture is synonymous with the removal of ornament from objects of daily use." He took pride that his own period was "incapable of producing new ornament," bragging, "we have out-grown ornament, we have struggled through to a state without ornament. Behold, the time is at hand, fulfilment awaits us. Soon the streets of the city will glow like white walls! Like Zion, the Holy City, the capital of heaven."

Taking a colonialist, Darwinian viewpoint, Loos transposed an evolutionary concept into a cultural sphere:

> In the womb the human embryo passes through all the development stages of the animal kingdom. At the moment of birth, human sensations are equal to those of a newborn dog. His childhood passes through all the transformations which correspond to the history of mankind. At the age of two, he sees like a Papuan, at four, like a Teuton, at six like Socrates, at eight like Voltaire. . . . The child is amoral. To us the Papuan is also amoral. The Papuan slaughters his enemies and devours them. He is no criminal. If, however, the modern man slaughters and devours somebody, he is a criminal or a degenerate. The Papuan tattoos his skin, his boat, his oar, in short, everything that is within his reach. He is no criminal. The modern man who tattoos himself is a criminal or a degenerate.[9]

Le Corbusier clearly borrowed Loos's ideas for his own rhetoric in *The Decorative Art of Today*:

> Decoration: baubles, charming entertainment for a savage. (And I do not deny that it is an excellent thing to keep an element of the savage alive in us—a small one.) But in the twentieth century our powers of judgement have developed greatly and we have raised our level of consciousness. Our spiritual needs are different, and higher worlds than those of decoration offer us commensurate experience. It seems justified to affirm: *the more cultivated a people becomes, the more decoration disappears*. (Surely it was Loos who put it so neatly.)[10]

One of the factors that made Le Corbusier, like a succession of other design reformers since the middle of the nineteenth century, so opposed to decoration was the way it had been used to hide flaws in the cheaply made, mass-produced objects that blanketed the marketplace during what he dubbed the "hurricane" of the machine age: "THE INDUSTRIALIST SAID," he wrote contemptuously, "'quite clearly, for an acceptable price I can only produce junk. But decoration will save me; let us cover *everything* with decoration. Let us hide the junk beneath decoration; decoration hides flaws, blemishes, all defects.' Desperate inspiration and commercial triumph."[11]

But decoration also impinged on the directly communicative aspect of simple, everyday forms, which he had admired in the work of Behrens and which he and Ozenfant elevated in their Purist paintings and discussed in their book *La Peinture moderne (Modern Painting)*. For their compositions, they chose ordinary, standardized, machine-made objects of daily use, identified through "*the law of mechanical selection*. This establishes that objects tend toward a type that is determined by the evolution of forms between the ideal of the greatest utility and that which satisfies the necessities of economic production, which conforms totally to natural laws." These were the most ordinary of objects having "the advantage of being perfectly legible and effortlessly recognizable. . . . What gives them a perfect legibility is the fact that they have always been made in the most universal, standard form."[12] They took these "type" objects for their subject matter, mainly bottles, pitchers, glasses, and other tableware that were perfectly legible and familiar to everyone (figs. 17, 18), painting them as immutable forms in even, local color, free from the effects of light or other ephemeral or accidental occurrences (fig. 19). These were archetypes, neutral objects whose destiny did not require the elaboration or ornamentation that had previously been expected of objects made for use in the home. Le Corbusier investigated this idea in a dialogue with himself:

> ". . . An object of use should be decorated; as our companion in fortune and adversity it should have a soul. Together, the souls of objects that have been decorated create an atmosphere of warmth which brightens our unhappy lot. The great emptiness of the machine age should be countered by the ineffable diffusion of a soothing and gently intoxicating decoration."
> *We protest.*
> *The objects of utility in our lives have freed the slaves of a former age. They are in fact themselves slaves, menials, servants. Do you want them as your soul-mates? We sit on them, work on them, make use of them, use them up; when used up, we replace them.*[13]

For Le Corbusier, chairs, bottles, baskets, shoes, and other similar items were not soul mates, they were tools required to satisfy the typical, basic necessities of life: "They are extensions of our limbs and are adapted to human functions that are type-functions. Type-needs, type-functions, therefore type-objects and type-furniture."[14]

In looking around at the decorative arts of his day, those objects designed for the use and enjoyment of individuals in the living rooms, dining rooms, studies, and bedrooms of their homes, Le Corbusier did not see much that responded to his idea of "type-objects" and "type-furniture." But he did identify many of these type characteristics in the world of industry and commerce, particularly those objects made for the efficiency of the modern office and factory, as well as in everyday mercantile items made for kitchen and work-room use: "type-objects, responding to type-needs: chairs to sit on, tables to work at, devices to give light, machines to write with (yes indeed!), racks to file things in."[15] In the chapter for which the book is named, he could give a praiseworthy assessment to a number of objects he found on the market that seemed to fulfill his vision of utility and order:

We notice among the products of industry articles of perfect convenience and utility, that soothe our spirits with the luxury afforded by the elegance of their conception, the purity of their execution, and the efficiency of their operation. They are so well thought out that we feel them to be harmonious, and this harmony is sufficient for our gratification.

And so . . . we have to ask ourselves whether these new objects do not suit us very well, and whether this rational perfection and precise formulation in each does not constitute sufficient common ground between them to allow the recognition of a *style*![16]

Such products, imbued in Le Corbusier's eyes with the harmony of the machine age, would furnish and ennoble the new architecture he envisioned as appropriate for society in the future, and it was with such industrially produced objects that Le Corbusier proceeded to furnish the Esprit Nouveau pavilion at the Paris Exposition of 1925. In choosing products with "rational perfection and precise formulation" that he found on the market (or his own versions made as prototypes for future industry) he hoped to bring together a nucleus of independent objects that in their totality would "allow the recognition of a *style*!"

NOTES

1. Amédée Ozenfant and Charles-Edouard Jeanneret, *Après le Cubisme*, 2nd ed. (Paris: Edition des Commentaires, 1918), 11; trans. in Susan L. Ball, *Ozenfant and Purism: The Evolution of a Style, 1915–1930* (Ann Arbor, Mich.: UMI Research Press, 1981), 35.
2. "Domaine de L'Esprit Nouveau," *L'Esprit Nouveau* 1 (1920).
3. Le Corbusier, *The Decorative Art of Today*, trans. James I. Dunnett (Cambridge, Mass.: MIT Press, 1987); originally published as *L'Art décoratif d'aujourd'hui* (Paris: Editions G. Crès et Cie, 1925).
4. Le Corbusier, *Towards a New Architecture*, trans. Frederick Etchells (London: John Rodker Publisher, 1927); originally published as *Vers une architecture* (Paris: Editions G. Crès et Cie, 1923).
5. *The Decorative Art of Today*, 84.
6. Ch.-E. Jeanneret, *Etude sur le mouvement d'art décoratif en Allemagne* (1912; reprint, New York: Da Capo Press, 1968).
7. *Le Corbusier: Les Voyages d'Allemagne, Carnets*, ed. Giuliano Gresleri (New York: The Monacelli Press, 1995), Carnet I, 42–43; transcription, 38.
8. Adolf Loos, "Ornement et Crime," *L'Esprit Nouveau* 2 (1920): 159–68.
9. Adolf Loos, "Ornament and Crime" (1908), in *The Architecture of Adolf Loos* (London: Arts Council of Great Britain, 1985), 100.
10. *The Decorative Art of Today*, 85.
11. Ibid., 54.
12. Amédée Ozenfant and Charles-Edouard Jeanneret, *La Peinture moderne* (Paris: Editions G. Crès et Cie, n.d.), 167–68.
13. *The Decorative Art of Today*, 1.
14. Ibid., 77, 79.
15. Ibid., 75.
16. Ibid., 91–93.

3

Furnishing the
Minimal Dwelling Unit

standardization

With the creation of the Esprit Nouveau pavilion at the Exposition Internationale des Arts Décoratifs et Industriels Modernes in Paris in 1925, Le Corbusier was able to bring to the public the ideas about modern housing and city planning that he had laid out in his book *Towards a New Architecture* and at the same time to test the concept of type furnishings that he had presented in *The Decorative Art of Today*. Following the contextual format of the small pavilions that were constructed for the display of objects in fully designed interiors, Le Corbusier and Pierre Jeanneret erected and furnished an actual two-story apartment unit, complete with a large enclosed terrace (fig. 20). For exhibition purposes, however, half of the side wall of the pavilion was painted like a billboard with the Esprit Nouveau emblem (fig. 21) and a circular addition was attached on the other side for the presentation of Le Corbusier's urban schemes. The pavilion was tucked away in a corner of the Grand Palais, a large, earlier exhibition building on the Right Bank of the Seine, screened by several other buildings and impossible to see from a distance. The Esprit Nouveau pavilion was "the most hidden of the exhibition" the invitation to its belated opening claimed,[1] although its placement was not necessarily the purposeful snub by the authorities that Le Corbusier maintained it was.

While the other pavilions were mostly elegant buildings conceived as temporary showpieces for unique, and generally extravagant, integrated ensembles designed to furnish homes with luxury items, the Esprit Nouveau pavilion had a completely different purpose: it was meant as a prototype for multiple, standardized units of mass housing, conceived as a minimal "dwelling type, of exclusively industrial execution, using a system of standard elements,"[2] and furnished with type objects also identified as suitable for mass distribution. The building was also unlike most of the other pavilions at the exhibition in its design aesthetic. It was a simple, unornamented, reinforced-concrete and glass structure while most of the others were more sculptural and complex, favoring a renewed classicism of form and bold, highly imaginative polychrome decoration (fig. 22). The exhibition was immensely successful in identifying a new French style of modern design, although as the apogee of what we now know as Art Deco, it did not, as popular understanding has it, offer only an orgy of Jazz Age ornament; rather, it included a vast range of stylistic interpretations, some highly ornamental and others quietly dignified, from those of decorative designers such as Süe et Mare, who reevaluated, interpreted, and updated eighteenth-century forms and ornament, to Robert Mallet-Stevens and Pierre Chareau, who, like Le Corbusier, thought in terms of reductive

20

design, however luxurious its materials might be. As restrained as the Esprit Nouveau pavilion was among the exuberance and decorative elaboration of much of the architecture at the exhibition, it soon achieved landmark status; it became the icon of modernism associated with the exhibition in Paris in 1925 just as Ludwig Mies van der Rohe's glass, steel, and marble German pavilion would signify modernism for the world's fair in Barcelona in 1929.

The Esprit Nouveau pavilion served as a model apartment for an urban building type that Le Corbusier had recently developed, what he called in French *immeubles-villas*, or apartment-homes. He saw each apartment as a separate unit, "in reality, a little house with a garden, no matter what level above the street it is situated at."[3] These individual house units, or "cells," joined on all sides by other identical *immeubles-villas*, were conceived as modules (not individual prefabricated elements) in a line of apartments with terraces (fig. 23) that theoretically could be repeated ad infinitum. This newly created urban structure formed the building blocks of his plan for a city of three million inhabitants, which he had unveiled at the Salon d'Automne in Paris in 1922 and presented again as a diorama in the pavilion's annex.

Three separate sources in the youthful experience of Le Corbusier, one structural, one spatial, and one conceptual, came together to define the *immeubles-villas* idea. The structure followed a scheme Le Corbusier had first developed

20 Esprit Nouveau pavilion, Paris, 1925, erected for the Exposition Internationale des Arts Décoratifs et Industriels Modernes. Fondation Le Corbusier, Paris. As described in the *Almanach d'architecture moderne*, "two entire walls of the terrace are painted dark burnt Sienna; the other wall and the ceiling are bright white. On the facades: light gray walls; the sliding metal screens are gray and pale ocher on the exterior, light blue on the interior." **21** Esprit Nouveau pavilion, side view. Fondation Le Corbusier, Paris. **22** Henri Sauvage. Printemps pavilion at the 1925 exhibition. From *L'Illustration* (1925).

21
22

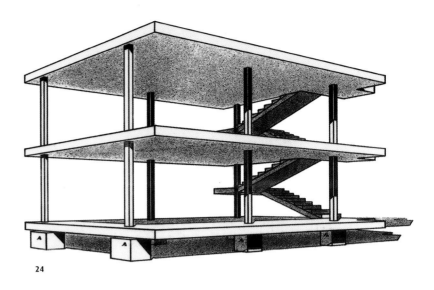

24

about 1914 in his design for the "Dom-ino" house (fig. 24), with a new type of skeletal-frame construction of reinforced concrete that formed the floors, supports, and stairs of a building and eliminated the need for load-bearing interior or exterior walls. With no internal divisions determined by structural requirements, the interior could develop freely. This allowed Le Corbusier to introduce his open- or free-plan design, and to create the large, open, modular spaces of the *immeubles-villas*. Le Corbusier's intention was to replicate apartment blocks made with the technology of the "Dom-ino" house in large numbers by fabricating them and their furnishings industrially, with virtually everything made in a factory and installed during construction "following standard measures and responding to a variety of needs," as he later explained: "windows, doors, standard storage units [*casiers*, literally "pigeon holes"] serving as cupboards, wardrobes, or other pieces of furniture and forming a part of the partition walls. One can envision a completely new method of construction: you hang the windows on the 'Dom-ino' skeleton; you affix the doors and their frames and align the cupboards forming the partitions. Then, at this moment only, do you begin to construct the exterior walls and the interior divisions."[4] Because it was a prototype, the Esprit Nouveau pavilion was not constructed with these factory methods that Le Corbusier envisioned, but its technology was industrial, and such elements as the modular system of sliding windows and the metal door frames made for the pavilion by the office furniture manufacturer Roneo were completely suited to serial manufacture.

The spatial configuration of the *immeubles-villas* was also an original proposal for domestic living. It had emerged from Le Corbusier and Jeanneret's encounters with vernacular design:

We were eating in a small restaurant, a cab drivers' hangout, in the center of Paris; there was a bar (of zinc), kitchen in the back; a gallery divided the height of the room; the front opened toward the street. One day we discovered this place and noticed that here were all the elements of an architectural mechanism that could be applied to the organization of a dwelling.
Simplification of light sources: a single large window at each end; two transverse bearing walls, a flat roof above; a box which could be used as a house. We dreamed of building this house throughout the country; the two walls would be of brick, stone, or masonry blocks, according to the availability of local materials. Only the cross-section reveals the standardized flooring system designed to be of reinforced concrete.[5]

The boxlike structure of this restaurant, open floor to ceiling except for the half balcony at the rear, gave rise to the "Citrohan" house, where half of the structure is given over to the double-height living space (fig. 25), as well as to the format of the pavilion with its long, double-height, open-plan living room, mezzanine bedrooms above (fig. 26), and a glass wall at one end.

But the conceptual model for an urban housing scheme that was at once private and communal, that is, private houses with gardens integrated structurally into a larger apartment block, had come even earlier, as an epiphany during Le Corbusier's student travels in Italy, and had affected him profoundly. In 1907, when he was in Florence and first visited the nearby Carthusian monastery of Galluzzo (or Ema, as it was known then, after the valley in which it was situated), he was struck by the unique building form that had developed centuries before to satisfy the particular needs

23 (pages 28, 29) Facade of the *immeubles-villas*, c. 1922. Ink. Fondation Le Corbusier, Paris (19.069). 24 "Dom-ino" house, showing its structural system of reinforced concrete, c. 1914. Ink, pencil, and colored pencil. Fondation Le Corbusier, Paris (19.209). The name "Dom-ino" was applied because the "footprint" of the six piers in the scheme looks like the markings on a domino, while the plan of the buildings mimics the placement of dominos during play. 25 Cross section of the "Citrohan" house, 1922. Ink. Fondation Le Corbusier, Paris (20.711). 26 Esprit Nouveau pavilion. Living room with view of balcony above. Musée des Arts Décoratifs, Paris.

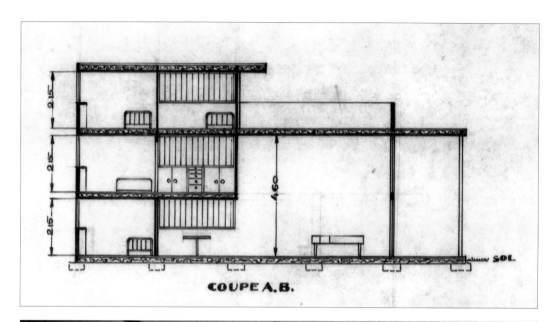

25
26

27

of the order. Based on isolation, not communal activity,[6] the Carthusian system required each monk to spend the week alone in contemplation and in work, tending a garden; only on Sundays and feast days did the monks join together for mass and meals in the refectory. In line with this way of life, the typical Carthusian monastery was constructed of a series of small attached houses of several rooms each, and each with a large enclosed garden, joined within a walled complex. The houses were protected from noise and from one another by double corridors (slits in the inner wall allowed food to be delivered during the week) and were connected to the outer wall of the complex by loggias with window-like openings at their ends through which the monks could view the surrounding countryside. This concept fascinated Le Corbusier; the garden and loggia became the focus of his recollections of the monastery, and this was one of the views of the complex that he sketched when he visited again several years later (fig. 27). His reaction to Galluzzo was immediate and intense: "Ah those Carthusians! I would like to live my entire life in what they call their cells," he wrote back to his teacher L'Eplattenier in 1907. "Here is the solution to the worker's house, an unparalleled model [*type*], or rather an earthly paradise."[7] The importance of his visits to Galluzzo cannot be overstated. Le Corbusier often acknowledged this as one of the formative experiences of his architectural education and as the basis for his *immeubles-villas* idea and the apartment houses developed from it that he built in France and Germany after the Second World War.

The Esprit Nouveau pavilion is known to us primarily through a series of photographs published by Le Corbusier in his *Almanach d'architecture moderne* in 1926,[8] and then frequently republished. A commemorative volume put together to give credit to the financial backers of the project and the firms that had worked on it, the *Almanach* was also an after-the-fact catalog of the pavilion. In it Le Corbusier both documented the concept of the building and explained his leap from the ideas explored in *The Decorative Art of Today* to the actuality of a prototype apartment furnished simply with type objects. For the Paris exhibition of 1925, "where everything *would be specific* and *where nothing would be typical*," he was determined, he wrote, "to attempt the arrangement of a home with standard furnishing elements, not those made for the enjoyment of an

art exhibition and for a public intent upon outdoing each other, but those fabricated industrially, existing in the world of commerce, without any artistic character provided by decoration overburdened with meaning. We wished to furnish our pavilion with industrial products in which the law of economy, commercial selection, was allowed to rule and to confer on these objects what one could call a style."[9] What we see in the photograph of the living room is a spare, lofty interior furnished by commercial selection; it contains only chairs, tables, and a system of storage cabinets (*casiers*)[10] —the three elements (aside from beds) that for Le Corbusier would suffice for furniture. "In fact," he proclaimed, "the house is nothing but cabinets on the one hand, chairs and tables on the other. The rest is an encumbrance."[11]

In attempting to outfit the pavilion with modern furnishing elements that would not encumber it, Le Corbusier first had to solve what he called "*the problem of the casiers*,"[12] that is, storage. Built-in closets of the type used in America were not customary in France, nor did a system of efficient, standard storage cabinets with the design he had in mind exist. Traditional decorating specified instead

a particular form of storage furniture for each room and each domestic function: sideboards and buffets for serving and for displaying and storing tableware, chests of drawers for linens and clothing, bookcases, desks, and wardrobes. Advocating interior spaces with multiple, varied uses, Le Corbusier sought to replace these heterogeneous pieces made for rooms with particular uses with cabinets of a universal form that would function equally well throughout the house. He opted for a regular system of compact, undifferentiated cabinets based on a standard format, which could be combined and superposed in different configurations. The *casiers* he designed, which originally were to have been manufactured in metal but ended up in the pavilion as wooden prototypes, exploited a module of rectangular units measuring 75 centimeters high, 150 centimeters long, and 35.5 centimeters deep—a measure he felt could easily contain most standard household objects. Assemblages of these modular units could be used singly against a wall or back to back in freestanding arrangements, which would then articulate spatial divisions. The upper floor of the pavilion had a large central spine made

28 Cabinets on the balcony of the Esprit Nouveau pavilion. Fondation Le Corbusier, Paris. An Innovation trunk is seen at the left. 29 Drawings for storage cabinets (*casiers*) for the Esprit Nouveau pavilion, c. 1925. Pencil and ink. Fondation Le Corbusier, Paris (29.802). 30 Dressing table unit from the Esprit Nouveau pavilion, 1925. Painted wood and mahogany veneer. Nationalmuseum, Stockholm. Shown closed and open, with bins pivoted outward as in the period photograph (fig. 28).

28

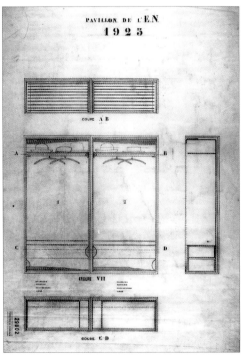

29

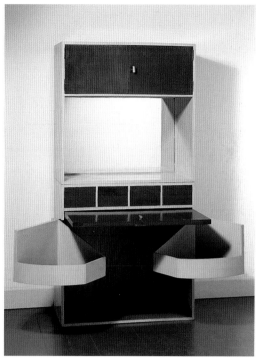

30

of them (fig. 28), creating a wide partition; it included four closet units (fig. 29), two wardrobes with adjustable shelves for folded clothing, one compartment for hats, and one for shoes, and had a dressing table at the end (fig. 30). A second *casier*, perpendicular to it, fitted with adjustable shelves, separated the bedroom from the dressing room. Three versions of the *casiers* were on the ground floor (fig. 31): two were freestanding double units (one with a fall-front desk, cupboards, and display compartments stood on tubular metal legs, and a taller unit like the one upstairs, sat on the floor), and the third was against the back wall (and also had a fall-front desk).

In creating these *casiers* Le Corbusier turned the conventional concept of storage completely around. Because he standardized the overall form of his cabinets into compact modules, he had to particularize their interiors so they could function as efficiently as the traditional pieces had. By surveying the sizes and uses of everyday objects—all sharing a commonality of measure, he said, because they were all based on human scale—he could outfit the interiors so that they were "meticulously fixed with the strictest economy of dimensions (arrangements for wardrobes, for underwear, for bedding, for shoes, hats, etc., for glassware, for different types of dishes; for kitchen equipment, for writing materials, for filing, etc.; for bookcases, for gramophone records, for the wireless, etc., etc.),"[13] with everything organized in an efficient fashion. This was a direction similar to that being followed by the Danish architect Kaare Klint, who early in the decade had begun to take statistical surveys of the sizes and shapes of everyday objects for the purpose of creating the most efficient storage arrangements possible. And this was the principle of a kitchen cabinet illustrated

in *L'Esprit Nouveau* in 1924 in an article on the modern functional style by Yves Labasque (fig. 32). Shelves, drawers, and partitions were created to fit exactly each type of item needed for table use: glassware, plates, bowls, bottles, tea service, napkins, and serving pieces. More important for Le Corbusier, however, was that by regularizing the *casiers* into simple rectangular units, he could integrate these furnishing elements into his grander architectural vision, for furniture of this type, he said, does not "add its potential architecture to an architecture already resolved. It makes architecture."[14]

Le Corbusier credited office furniture and the fitted wardrobes and steamer trunks sold by the Innovation company, as well as the "ingenious, bold, and elegant" furniture of the Parisian designer Francis Jourdain, as his inspiration for the strict modularity and precise interior arrangements of his cabinets.[15] These antecedents had all put organizational functions based on standard measures and usage above aesthetics of form, decoration, and style: standard paper formats determined the sizes of the drawers and compartments of office desks and filing cabinets, apparel types determined the dimensions of each of the specialized compartments of Innovation trunks and wardrobes, and the basic needs of household arrangements determined the format of Jourdain's modular, interchangeable furniture.

Office furniture was a model that Le Corbusier frequently cited (fig. 33). This new system of filing "which clarifies our needs," he wrote, "has an effect on the lay-out of rooms, and of buildings. We have only to introduce this method into our apartments and decorative art will meet its destiny: type-furniture and architecture."[16] A more important, direct source for his type units, however, was the example

31

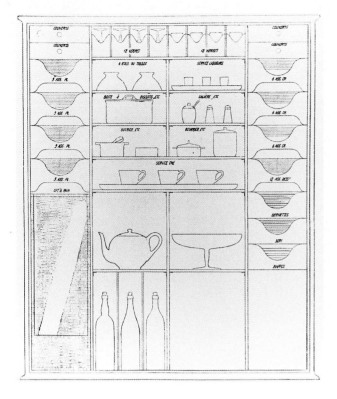

32
33

of Innovation, an American company founded in 1898, with branches in London and Paris. Innovation took a creative approach to organization that was aimed at simplifying the problems of storing clothing both in wardrobes at home and in the large trunks used at that time for traveling. The firm promoted a compulsion for compactness and order, and its advertising was meant to astound with detailed annotations of the type, and the large number of each type, of clothing that could be conveniently stored in each drawer and hanging compartment (fig. 34). Between 1923 and 1925, the firm placed a series of advertisements in *L'Esprit Nouveau*, which Le Corbusier designed himself, that pointed out the advances of the company's products. In one, he showed the advantage of the Innovation system, comparing a dark, period-style room encumbered by a traditional freestanding wardrobe with a bright, spacious, modern one fitted out with organized built-in storage from Innovation and no extraneous furniture (fig. 35). He went so far as to display an Innovation steamer trunk next to his *casiers* in the Esprit Nouveau pavilion to emphasize the pedigree of his storage design and to demonstrate their connection as type objects (see fig. 28). In an addendum to the *Almanach,* in which Le Corbusier outlined the new industrial processes and materials that had been used in the pavilion, he showered high praise on the firm, which, by rejecting the styles of the past and by eschewing luxurious materials and techniques in manufacturing utilitarian goods, offered, he said, "objects of a new beauty" that were "truly the *modern decorative art*."[17]

Le Corbusier's early concern with solving storage problems architecturally and his adaptation of Innovation's organizing systems are documented in studies for the remodeling of the Villa Berque in Paris in 1921–22, a project about which very little is known. Annotations to a drawing for a cabinet with a rounded profile and moldings that he designed for this house (fig. 36) specify compartments meant to hold "5 Innovation drawers." It was in drawings for this house, also, that he seems for the first time to have employed a storage unit architecturally as a room divider, in this case a two-sided cabinet with many drawers and open display areas, which was set perpendicular to the wall to divide the expanse of

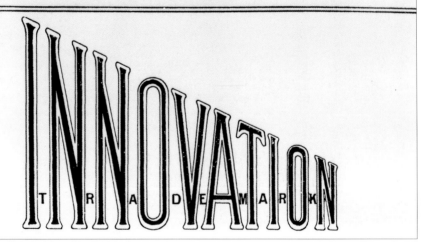

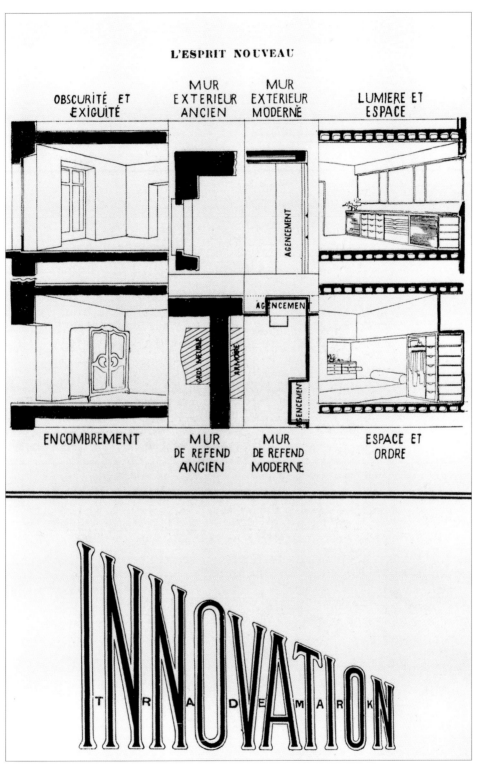

L'ESPRIT NOUVEAU

OBSCURITÉ ET EXIGUITÉ — MUR EXTERIEUR ANCIEN — MUR EXTERIEUR MODERNE — LUMIERE ET ESPACE

ENCOMBREMENT — MUR DE REFEND ANCIEN — MUR DE REFEND MODERNE — ESPACE ET ORDRE

INNOVATION
TRADEMARK

36 Sketch for a cabinet for the Villa Berque, Paris, 1921–22. Pencil, colored pencil, and ink. Fondation Le Corbusier, Paris (9.330). **37** Sketches of the living room of the Villa Berque, dated 1921. Ink. Fondation Le Corbusier, Paris (9.316). **38** Sketch for the living-dining room of the *immeubles-villas*, dated 1922. Ink. Fondation Le Corbusier, Paris (19.097).

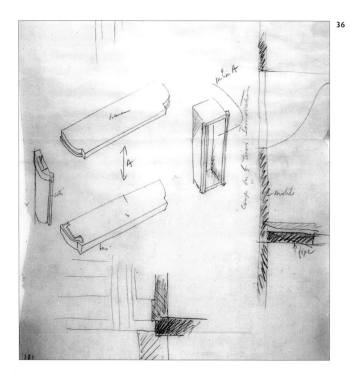

36

a large, boldly curved, open-plan living room (fig. 37). About the same time he also drew a fitted storage piece as a room divider in an interior sketch for the *immeubles-villas*—separating living room and dining room (fig. 38)—but he had not yet arrived at the prototypical *casiers* with the modular, undifferentiated format that he created for the Esprit Nouveau pavilion in 1925.

The third influence on storage cited by Le Corbusier, that of Francis Jourdain, a painter and designer eleven years Le Corbusier's senior, socially progressive and with wide connections in French reform circles,[18] was considerably broader. From the first decade of the century, when the florid tracery of the Art Nouveau style was still captivating Paris, Jourdain designed rectilinear, rationalized furniture that was free of ornament, with much of it directed to the possibility of production for workers with modest incomes. With the foundation of his own workshop, Les Ateliers Modernes, in 1912, Jourdain went on to manufacture his furniture designs as well (fig. 39). At the Salon d'Automne in Paris in 1913, Jourdain exhibited the interiors he had created for his own Paris apartment, outfitted with interchangeable furniture designed and manufactured in his own atelier. He integrated the various storage forms, such as sideboards, bookcases, and dressers, into one system suitable for use in any room of the house. These interiors introduced his space-saving concept that eliminated most of the freestanding furniture (except tables and chairs), much as Le Corbusier was to do in 1925, when he claimed that "the rest is an encumbrance." Jourdain's designs were the first important French contribution to standardized type furniture, which

was being more fully investigated in Germany during the first two decades of the century with the *Typenmöbel* systems of such architects as Richard Riemerschmid and Bruno Paul, a concept much supported by the Werkbund. In an advertisement in *Les Cahiers d'Aujourd'hui*, Jourdain also acknowledged his indebtedness to the works of Adolf Loos for the simplicity, clarity, proportions, and ingenuity of his modern interiors.[19]

The young architect Charles-Edouard Jeanneret had seen Jourdain's display in Paris in 1913 and on his return to Switzerland wrote him an enthusiastic fan letter:

> I had gone to Paris for three days to visit the Salon d'Automne. Very concerned with the problem of interior decoration, I wanted to calm my growing doubts with the various exhibitions of Parisian artists. I hoped to find a path to follow or at least a choice, to become enchanted and thus experience change or conversion. I had great hopes, was enchanted with the first things I saw, then quickly became tired with the whole thing and disconcerted. . . . Nevertheless, I went away with one lasting impression: that of your work at the Salon d'Automne. And indeed this was a surprise because I did not expect to feel such delight.[20]

Le Corbusier's accord with the principles of logic and the universality of Jourdain's furniture would be demonstrated in his later work, and there is no doubt about the lasting impression of his visit to the Salon in 1913.

As furnishing for the pavilion, Le Corbusier chose two types of seating, a comfortable upholstered easy chair of the

39 Francis Jourdain. Interiors with interchangeable furniture, 1912–13. Ink. Musée d'Art et d'Histoire, Saint-Denis.

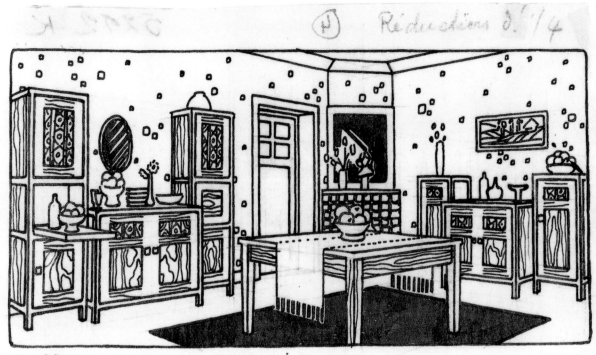

salle a manger

cabinet de travail

39

studio

cabinet de toilette

40 Page from Maple & Co. catalog, c. 1925. The Winterthur Library, Delaware: Printed Books and Periodical Collection. **41** Thonet bentwood chairs. From *L'Esprit Nouveau* (1924). **42** Esprit Nouveau pavilion. Terrace. Fondation Le Corbusier, Paris. The sliding screen panels are seen at right.

kind he associated with Maple and Co., an English decorating firm with a branch in Paris (fig. 40), and a light, open, caned, bentwood armchair of the kind developed in the nineteenth century by the Austrian firm Thonet (fig. 41). The Maple-style and Thonet chairs (as well as the wiry metal ones he selected for the pavilion's terrace, designs ubiquitous in the parks of Paris; fig. 42) are his textbook examples of applying the law of "commercial selection" to the furnishing of domestic interiors. Le Corbusier admired them for the way their forms had been refined over a long period of time to satisfy their purpose and reduced to the essentials of their manufacture. He extolled their virtues as types in a footnote to his chapter "Type-Needs, Type-Furniture," which he may have added to the broad, polemical text in anticipation of the use of the chairs in the pavilion: "During the long and scrupulous process of development in the factory," he explained, "the Thonet chair gradually takes on its final weight and thickness, and assumes a format that allows good connections; this process of perfecting by almost imperceptible steps is the same as that to which an engine is subjected, whose poetry is to run well—and cheaply. The Maple[']s armchair, which is attuned to our movements and quick to respond to them, assumes an ever more distinctive profile."[21] Here then are his own examples of the chair as a "machine for sitting in."

Le Corbusier tells us in the *Almanach* that he introduced in the pavilion "the humble Thonet bentwood armchair, certainly the most common as well as the cheapest of armchairs . . . of which millions of examples furnish our continent and the two Americas."[22] This simple model, designed for use by workers in offices and other commercial establishments, first appeared in Thonet catalogs around 1902 and had, as Le Corbusier reported, sold extremely well throughout the world. Side by side with it was the Maple-style armchair (see fig. 31), a fully upholstered form, which had a totally different function. It had also evolved decades earlier, in England, where, exuding the idea of comfort, it had become a standard furnishing in gentlemen's clubs. Le Corbusier had obtained club chairs of this type, the Franklin and Newstead models, from Maple for his other building and decorating projects under way at the same time. These had been sent back to a client in La Chaux-de-Fonds and to the villa he was completing in Auteuil for Raoul La Roche.[23] But he had to go elsewhere for the pavilion's chairs because, as he explained, the large Maple models did not fit through the narrow, 66-centimeter-wide door of the pavilion. Le Corbusier ordered five smaller (and cheaper) versions from the firm of Abel Motté, a supplier in Paris whose letterhead read, "Manufacturer of Comfortable English Chairs—Modern

Siège Thonet (inventeur du bois courbé).

and Period,"[24] reflecting the popularity that the English style was then enjoying in France. Motté copied these stuffed chairs for the pavilion, delivering them under the same English names used by Maple.[25] Motté made various chairs of this type, and four photographs he sent to Le Corbusier some years later, annotated with their measurements (fig. 43), show several of the styles that Le Corbusier would have been able to select for his buildings.

Some critics have seen an irony in Le Corbusier's practical solution to supplying type-objects by designing his own (such as the *casiers*, when appropriate ones were not yet available), or by ordering custom-made equivalents (such as smaller, more compact club chairs, because of the narrow "standard" doorways of the pavilion).[26] But this is a misunderstanding of Le Corbusier's concept of type, which was not tied to any one designer or manufacturer. Even when he identified his type designs as Maple or Thonet products, Le Corbusier considered them generic models, to be made in different sizes and materials by a host of different manufacturers who would eventually supply the entire world with standardized furnishings on an industrial model.

42

The tables used in the pavilion, supplied by a manufacturer of hospital equipment, were of two designs, both set on tubular metal legs and both adaptable for several uses. One had a removable laminated mahogany top and the other was of fixed metal (on the terrace were two cement tables built into the architecture). "We have created tables," Le Corbusier wrote in the *Almanach*, "whose dimensions obey a law of combination and which are neither tables for the dining room nor for the parlor. We have noted how they can be transported easily from one room to the other. Thus a removable top in excellent lamination and a rigid, light metal frame. Such tables can be used as a desk or a tea table, and by putting them together, banquets can be served on them."[27] This flexible concept had already been seen in the work of Francis Jourdain, who much earlier had made similar use of combinable tables in the first complete interior he designed, in Paris in 1906.[28]

The accessories displayed on the tables and in the shelves and compartments of the *casiers*, industrial products of white ceramic and clear glass, such as test tubes, crucibles, and mortars bought from manufacturers of laboratory equipment and used as vases and planters (see figs. 26, 28), were likewise statements about type. These simple undecorated pieces had the imprimatur of long use, very much like the everyday tableware that Ozenfant and Le Corbusier selected as subjects for their Purist compositions. For many of the pavilion's visitors, these mundane, industrial objects "manifested an acute modernism," Le Corbusier reported. "Their material was the most simple, the most rudimentary, the most pure; their shapes were precise, corresponding to function."[29]

Two unique symbolic items, a large globe and a model airplane (see fig. 31), were included among the furnishings of the Esprit Nouveau pavilion to emphasize its universality and its modernity. Similarly, on the walls of the pavilion, which were uninterrupted by moldings of any kind, and amid the type furnishings bought from commercial sources, Le Corbusier introduced modern works of art: Cubist paintings by Picasso, Braque, Léger, and Gris; Purist paintings that he and Ozenfant had created; and Cubist sculpture by Jacques Lipchitz. In doing so, he completed the visualization of his rhetoric in *The Decorative Art of Today*: "If decorative art has no reason to exist, tools [type furnishings] on the other hand do exist, and there exist also architecture and the work of art."[30] Cubist paintings had been shown in a contemporary interior setting in Paris a decade earlier, in an installation known as the "Cubist House" at the Salon d'Automne of 1912, organized by the decorator André Mare. In this installation, a faceted, Cubistic, plaster facade

designed by the sculptor Raymond Duchamp-Villon opened into three rooms decorated with walls and furniture in bright colors and filled with Cubist art. One was called a "bourgeois living room," a generic designation used without any sense of irony or condescension, which suggested that avant-garde paintings of this style might well find an audience within middle-class households.[31] The Esprit Nouveau module was not, however, intended as middle-class housing but as a standardized apartment for workers. Yet it too was furnished with Cubist art. Where would Le Corbusier find millions of high-minded standard humans to live in these factory-like houses, people who would reject the ornamental furniture in historical styles that they aspired to for a home filled with austere industrial objects chosen by commercial selection, people who would derive satisfaction from such challenging works of art? One answer would come from a German critic who questioned the intent of two similar buildings that Le Corbusier and Jeanneret constructed at the Weissenhof experimental housing exhibition in Stuttgart two years later. The inhabitants would not be workers but intellectuals and individualists, he concluded, "those individualists who—untrammeled by 'historical ballast,' unsentimental, footloose, nowhere at home, free of all ties—might want to inhabit such a nomadic tent of concrete and glass." True, he admitted, "the intellectual is one form of today's humanity; but is he *the* type, whose needs and aspirations are to determine the form of home building that will go into mass production and cater for mass need?"[32]

As seen in the photographs, the Cubist and Purist paintings seem to dominate the pavilion's interior, and the furnishings—casually placed, disparate objects that relate to each other seemingly only in the simplicity of their outlines—appear almost lost. What is absent from these photographs (but not from Le Corbusier's description of the pavilion in the *Almanach*) and what brought the interior together as a composition was its color, chosen according to Purist tenets. Despite the rhetoric in *The Decorative Art of Today* about the blessings that would be derived from an edict to whitewash all the interiors of Paris (probably more a statement about starting design again from scratch than a polemic about color),[33] Le Corbusier united the white walls of the pavilion with those that were colored. He claimed to use color to emphasize spatial, architectural qualities, not decorative ones, based on research into the physics of color: "Color which modifies the walls according to whether they are in full light or in shadow can lead the eye through the intricate spaces created by the plan and expand the vibrant impression of space: red retains its qualities only in full light; blue vibrates in the shade, etc.: physicality of color. . . . One can compose architecturally on those bases: The 'whitewash' gleams on account of this bare wall which is somber (burnt or raw umber), of this wall which is hot (ochers), of this wall which recedes (blues, etc.). Entirely white, the house would be a jug of cream."[34] Because the Esprit Nouveau pavilion was demolished after the close of the exhibition, exact knowledge of its distinct coloration has been lost, but a good idea of how it looked was recaptured in a furnished reconstruction of part of the main floor (fig. 44). In this view, the dynamic of the green earth tones of the walls and the reddish brown upholstery of the chair plays off similar tones in the paintings and the geometric and African tribal carpets to bring visual unity to the interior. The furniture itself—*casiers* painted yellow ocher, some with doors of mahogany veneer; tables of white and gray; bentwood chairs painted gray; and club chairs upholstered in reddish leather—also held a more significant role in the ensemble than could have been imagined from the black and white photographs alone.

The Esprit Nouveau pavilion was not completed until July 1925, three months after the rest of the exhibition opened to the public. Le Corbusier was bitterly disappointed when it did not receive a grand prize for architecture, the highest level of award given, which in the tradition of such exhibitions was handed out by the hundreds. According to Le Corbusier, one of the vice presidents of the jury, the French engineer and architect Auguste Perret (with whom Le Corbusier had apprenticed some fifteen years earlier), opposed the jury's own recommendation for the grand prize with the opinion that the pavilion had "no architecture."[35] As absurd as it might seem to condemn Le Corbusier's work for having "no architecture," a casual visitor to the pavilion might well have agreed with Perret, for the building was only a fragment of a much bolder architectural endeavor: it was not firmly set on the ground and had no distinguishable facade or formal entranceway; moreover, a circular addition was rudely stuck onto its side. Its most memorable exterior feature was accidental: the ad hoc circle cut out of the roof above the terrace to accommodate a tree that the architect was not allowed to cut down.

Le Corbusier reported in the *Oeuvre complète* in 1929 that he was convinced from the beginning that the exhibition's building committee was antagonistic to him and "made use of its powers to evince the most marked hostility to the execution of my scheme,"[36] to the extent of raising an 18-foot-high barricade to hide it from view (although the fence may very well have been erected solely for visitor safety since the pavilion was so late in reaching completion). In his "Brève Histoire des nos tribulations" ("A Short History

43

of Our Trials"), which had been intended for publication in 1926 as an appendix to the *Almanach* but was suppressed for reasons of tact and did not appear in print until 1948 as an article in a special issue of *L'Architecture d'Aujourd'hui* devoted to his work,[37] he recounted a whole series of slights and impediments that had been put in the way of his completion of the pavilion. This he saw as a battle of generations dating back a decade, a reaction against his theoretical writings and his controversial Salon proposal for a city of three million inhabitants. But much of the opposition may also have been caused by the extraordinary size of the pavilion he projected, the unusual details of his flat-roofed, standardized structure, and, later, the delays in beginning construction caused by his lack of funds. Le Corbusier, always self-righteous, tried to emphasize his position as a unique—and persecuted—"modern" architect through his choice of illustrations for the article, in which photographs of the Esprit Nouveau pavilion were paired with images of the most highly ornamental objects and pavilions, as if there had been only two extremes of design at the exhibition.

With the reiteration of his complaints in the preface to the 1959 edition of *The Decorative Art of Today*, the affair was transformed into a "scandal" for the postwar period, grist for the modernist critics who enjoyed enlarging on Le Corbusier's reputation as a misunderstood genius. In his *Master Builders*, Peter Blake embellished the story still further, reporting that "the hatred for Corbu's pavilion was passionate and vitriolic."[38] Opinion was indeed divided, but

not to that extent. A number of French critics, such as Le Corbusier's sparring partner Léandre Vaillat, were disturbed by the standardized solution to interior design he proposed, which they viewed suspiciously as Germanic (ignoring, to Le Corbusier's continual consternation, that the Jeanneret family had solid French roots):

> If this pavilion is in the author's intention a demonstration to teach the public, which has forgotten it, the supremacy of construction over ornamentation, then I approve of it, with the reservation that none of this is so new that one wishes it affirmed for us; but if he intends to persuade us, with a forcefulness that has nothing persuasive about it, that a house is a "machine for living," no. A house is not a factory where one works and where, in order to earn a little paper money, one performs a few mechanical gestures, always the same. A house, to be sure, must be answerable to logic, reason, and good sense, and we find, thank God! enough of these qualities in our national and regional traditions, without seeking them in German-Swiss rationalism.[39]

But many positive reactions also appeared. Not only did the avant-garde critics of such magazines as *Architecture Vivante*, published by his friend Jean Badovici, give support to Le Corbusier's work, but even the official reports of the exhibition, issued in 1926 as the *Encyclopédie des arts décoratifs et industriels modernes aux XXème siècle*, found merit in his design, and an illustration of the pavilion was included in this twelve-volume work.[40] While acknowledging its fragmentary nature and similarly raising doubts that the "cell" concept could possibly find acceptance in France, the *Encyclopédie* allowed that "in spite of its strange appearance, it was very much of this world, an industrial world, not a utopian realm. . . . This concept, in spite of its excesses, is something to reflect upon and for unbiased observers it can open up new perspectives."

In his anger over the loss of a grand prize for the pavilion, Le Corbusier never seems to have acknowledged that he and Pierre Jeanneret individually received diplomas of honor (the second highest category of awards) in the architecture category. Rather than being singled out for rejection because of the modernity of their work, the partners received the same award given to a number of other modernist architects, including the Dutch firm Bijvoet & Duiker, the German Peter Behrens, and the Austrian Oskar Strnad. The pavilion's furnishings ranked much lower in their class, however, winning only a silver medal (the fourth of six prize categories, and the same award given to the standardized, geometric, painted wooden fittings of Alexander

Rodchenko's "Workers Club" in the USSR pavilion).[41] Le Corbusier could hardly have expected to do much better in this area, having proudly boasted in the *Almanach* that his furnishings, in which the "law of economy, commercial selection, was allowed to rule," were "in flagrant contradiction" with the regulations of the exposition.[42] These rules admitted only "works of new inspiration and a true originality. . . . Copies, imitations, and forgeries of earlier styles" were "rigorously excluded."[43] While Le Corbusier did not lean on earlier styles, and the *casiers* he designed were definitely "of new inspiration," the other pieces—the Maple-type chairs, bentwood chairs, and laboratory items—were neither "new" nor "of a true originality."

Le Corbusier's strategy of commercial selection followed an approach that had been promoted at the end of the previous century by Adolf Loos in a series of articles in the Viennese newspaper *Neue Freie Presse*. Recalling his youth, Loos explained that then "one decorated his home the way one outfits himself today. We buy our shoes from the shoemaker, coats, pants, and waistcoat from the tailor, collars and cuffs from the shirtmaker, hats from the hatter, walking stick from the turner. None of them knows any of the others, and yet everything matches quite nicely."[44] For Loos, "the common bond that ties all of the furniture in one room together consists in the fact that the owner has made the selection."[45] Le Corbusier adopted this same shopping mentality for his pavilion, relying on his selection of simple objects expressive of the spirit of their own time to create a modern, unified ensemble. After a century of ornamentalism, Le Corbusier found that pure, simple, and basic forms "manifested an acute modernism" for visitors to the pavilion. Supported by his rhetoric and by the context of the pavilion, the simple furnishings came to be considered "modern," regardless of the fact that unornamented design (from Georgian silver to vernacular and Shaker furniture, and Victorian utilitarian objects) belongs to a recurrent stylistic pattern that is in itself historically neutral. But Le Corbusier reversed the lesson of history and succeeded in claiming simplicity for modernity with simple furnishings and "good taste manifested by choice, suitability, proportion, and harmony."[46] By its context alone his disparate ensemble was made to seem modern then, and through the continuing insistence on his principles of decoration, and the continued availability of the kinds of objects he ennobled as types—Thonet chairs, industrial ceramics, comfortable stuffed armchairs—it still seems modern today.

NOTES

1. Reproduced in Le Corbusier, *The Decorative Art of Today*, trans. James I. Dunnett (Cambridge, Mass.: MIT Press, 1987), xvi.
2. Fondation Le Corbusier, Paris, archives (hereafter FLC) A2-13-86.
3. *Le Corbusier et Pierre Jeanneret: Oeuvre complète de 1910–1929*, ed. W. Boesiger and O. Stonorov, 4th ed. (Zurich: Les Editions d'Architecture Erlenbach, 1946), 41.
4. Ibid., 23–24.
5. Ibid., 31; *Le Corbusier 1910–60* (New York: G. Wittenborn, 1960), 25 (translation modified).
6. See Wolfgang Braunfels, *Monasteries of Western Europe: The Architecture of the Orders* (Princeton, N.J.: Princeton University Press, 1972), 111–24.
7. Le Corbusier to Charles L'Eplattenier, September 15, 1907; quoted in Mary Patricia May Sekler, *The Early Drawings of Charles-Edouard Jeanneret (Le Corbusier), 1902–1908* (New York and London: Garland Publishing, 1977), 192.
8. Le Corbusier, *Almanach d'architecture moderne* (Paris: Les Editions G. Crès et Cie, 1926).
9. Ibid., 145.
10. The furnishings are extensively documented by Arthur Rüegg in "Le Pavillon de L'Esprit Nouveau en tant que Musée Imaginaire," in *L'Esprit Nouveau: Le Corbusier et l'industrie 1920–1925* (Strasbourg: Les Musées de Ville de Strasbourg, 1987), 134–51.
11. *Almanach d'architecture moderne*, 111.
12. Ibid., 145.
13. Ibid., 112.
14. Ibid., 145.
15. Ibid., 113.
16. *The Decorative Art of Today*, 77.
17. *Almanach d'architecture moderne*, 196.
18. Jourdain (1876–1958) was the son of Frantz Jourdain, a noted architect. Through his close friendship with the founder of the journal *Les Cahiers d'Aujourd'hui*, he was responsible for the publication of the French translation of Adolf Loos's modernist tract "Ornament and Crime" in the magazine in 1913, predating by almost a decade its publication in *L'Esprit Nouveau*. For Jourdain, see Suzanne Tise, "Jourdain," in Arlette Barré-Despond, *Jourdain* (New York: Rizzoli, 1991), 213–343.
19. See Tise, ibid. 255.
20. Charles-Edouard Jeanneret to Francis Jourdain, December 21, 1913, Bibliothèque de La Chaux-de-Fonds; trans. in ibid., 252.
21. *The Decorative Art of Today*, 76n.
22. *Almanach d'architecture moderne*, 145.
23. Le Corbusier to Maple & Co., Paris, order of February 4, 1925, FLC. French retailers also used English names for this type of furniture; see Nancy J. Troy, *Modernism and the Decorative Arts in France: Art Nouveau to Le Corbusier* (New Haven, Conn., and London: Yale University Press, 1991), 213, fig. 153.
24. See, for example, bill of June 26, 1925, FLC A2-14-117.
25. Maple & Co., Paris, to M. La Roche, bill of March 20, 1925, FLC P5-1-269.
26. See, for example, Mary McLeod, "Architecture or Revolution: Taylorism, Technocracy, and Social Change," *Art Journal* 43 (1983): 141.
27. *Almanach d'architecture moderne*, 145.
28. See Tise, op. cit., fig. 107.
29. *Almanach d'architecture moderne*, 168–69.
30. *The Decorative Art of Today*, 118.
31. The Cubist House is thoroughly discussed by Troy, op. cit., 79–96.
32. Edgar Wedepohl, *Wasmuth's Monatshefte für Baukunst* 8 (1927): 396–97; trans. in Karin Kirsch, *The Weissenhofsiedlung: Experimental Housing Built for the Deutscher Werkbund,*

44 Reconstruction of the living room of the Esprit Nouveau pavilion with original furniture and paintings (by Arthur Rüegg and Silvio Schmed, 1987). Furnishings include a Maple-type leather armchair, bentwood chair, tubular metal table, paintings by Juan Gris and Amédée Ozenfant, and a relief by Jacques Lipchitz.

44

Stuttgart, 1927 (New York: Rizzoli, 1998), 117.
33. See "A Coat of Whitewash, The Law of Ripolin," in *The Decorative Art of Today*, 185–92.
34. *Almanach d'architecture moderne*, 146.
35. Preface to the 1959 edition, *The Decorative Art of Today*, xv.
36. *Le Corbusier et Pierre Jeanneret: Oeuvre complète de 1910–1929*, ed. W. Boesiger and O. Stonorov, 4th ed. (Zurich: Les Editions d'Architecture Erlenbach, 1946), 104.
37. Le Corbusier, "Brève Histoire des nos tribulations," *L'Architecture d'Aujourd'hui* (April 1948): 59–67.
38. Peter Blake, *The Master Builders* (New York: Alfred A. Knopf, 1960), 45.
39. Léandre Vaillat, "La Tendance internationale à l'exposition des arts décoratifs," *L'Illustration* 4313 (1925); trans. in McLeod, op. cit., 144.
40. See *Encyclopédie des arts décoratifs et industriels modernes aux XXème siècle*, vol. 2, *Architecture* (1926; reprint, New York and London: Garland Publishing, 1977), 45–46, pl. LXV.
41. Exposition Internationale des Arts Décoratifs et Industriels Modernes, Paris, *Liste des récompenses* (Paris: Imprimerie des Journaux Officiels, 1926), Classe 1, Architecture, 4–9; Classe 7, Ensembles de Mobiliers, 15–18.
42. *Almanach d'architecture moderne*, 145.
43. Exposition Internationale des Arts Décoratifs et Industriels Modernes, Paris, *Règlement*, Titre II: Conditions Générales d'Admission, Article 4.
44. Adolf Loos, "Interiors: A Prelude," in *Spoken into the Void: Collected Essays 1897–1900*, trans. Jane O. Newman and John H. Smith (Cambridge, Mass.: MIT Press, 1982), 19. These articles were reprinted in 1921 by Georges Crès, Le Corbusier's publisher in Paris.
45. Adolf Loos, "Interiors in the Rotonda," in ibid., 24.
46. *The Decorative Art of Today*, 79.

4

Outfitting the
New Architecture

individualization

In creating and outfitting private houses, the major source of income for his firm during the 1920s,[1] Le Corbusier turned from the abstractions and rhetoric of type housing and type objects that dominated his thinking for *The Decorative Art of Today* and the Esprit Nouveau pavilion to consider the practicalities of specific sites and the needs of individual clients. As much as he could, he maintained the position of architect in control (some might have said out of control, since numerous delays, technological hitches, and cost overruns dogged most of these projects), with clients generally beholden to him not only for the shape of their houses but also for the suitability of the decoration and the furnishings within. The young Swiss banker Raoul La Roche was among the most amenable and the most adoring of all Le Corbusier's clients, dependent on the architect for the formation of an exemplary collection of Cubist and Purist paintings as well as for his singular living quarters in Paris; in the end he was willing to accept almost any of the architect's ideas and almost any inconvenience to sustain the relationship that brought him the "poem of walls" in which he lived.[2] At the other extreme were the Ternisiens, he a musician, she an artist, whose relationship with the firm went sour and who were later written off with disdain: "The problem rigorously stated by them was to eliminate all . . . superfluities," Le Corbusier explained to a lawyer about their villa in Boulogne as the legal battles brought on by their financial difficulties dragged on, "but as soon as the house was built, our clients filled it up with unbelievable bric-a-brac which had nothing in common with the house itself or indeed the very principles of our architecture."[3] Clients on the whole must have had a good idea of what they were letting themselves in for when they commissioned their houses from this most demanding of designers, and it was surely the thrill of being in the forefront of modern architecture rather than a search for conventional comfort that sent them to Le Corbusier in the first place. And, indeed, the names Cook, Church, La Roche, Savoye, and Stein are now attached to what have become icons of Corbusian—and twentieth-century—modernism, crisp, concrete boxes that exemplify Le Corbusier's "Five Points of a New Architecture," which he first articulated in 1927: houses raised on columns (*pilotis*), with flat roofs planted as gardens, open plans, facades that were no longer weight bearing and could be freely composed, and strip, or ribbon, windows.

As much as Le Corbusier preached standardization, these houses were totally individualized for their sites and the situations of their clients, even if they shared concepts and technology with those of his minimal dwelling units, and even if he could convert his unique designs into modular elements for future standardized housing units, as he did in his scheme for building seventeen identical versions of the Villa Savoye (fig. 45) in a high-class housing development near Buenos Aires (fig. 46). Unlike the "Citrohan" house and the Esprit Nouveau cell, with their simple, regular, box-like typology and transparent schema, these buildings were complex affairs, visually incomprehensible until clarified by traversing the entire structure. It was with these projects that Le Corbusier first developed his concept of the architectural promenade, a controlled climb along twisting and turning ramps and staircases that open onto set vistas and reveal calculated moments of visual excitement finally to arrive at the apex of the building, most often a roof terrace, where the interior experience of architecture as man's supreme artistic creation melds with the exterior experience of nature as God's supreme spiritual creation.

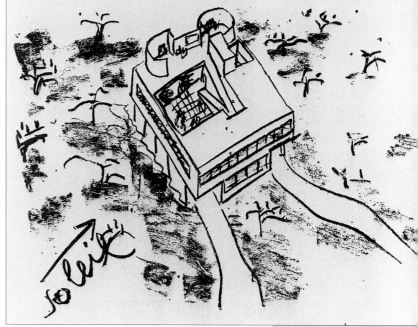

45

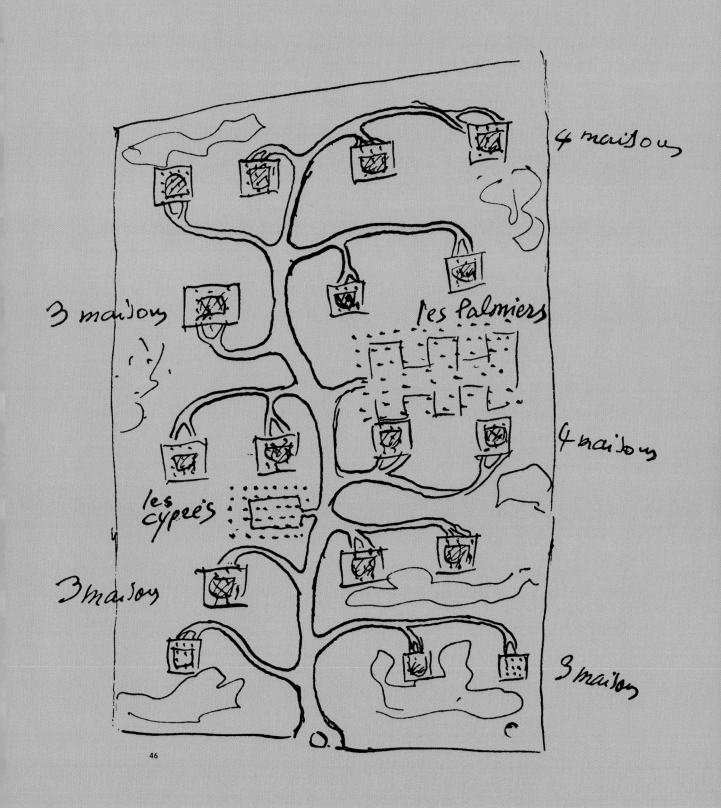

4 maisons

les Palmiers

3 maisons

4 maisons

les cyprès

3 maisons

3 maisons

46

45 Villa Savoye. From *Précisions* (1930). **46** Project for the adaptation of the Villa Savoye housing type to a development of seventeen houses in a meadow near Buenos Aires. From *Précisions* (1930).

47 48 49 50 The villas of Raoul La Roche and Albert and Lotti Jeanneret, Paris, 1923–25. From *Almanach d'architecture moderne* (1926). 51 Villa La Roche. Garden seen from hall. 52 Villa La Roche. Hall. 53 Villa La Roche. Staircase seen from hall.

47 48 49 50

The architect's intent is no better shown than in a sequence of photographs published in his *Almanach d'architecture moderne* documenting the two attached houses in the Auteuil section of Paris that he designed and built for his brother and sister-in-law, Albert and Lotti Jeanneret, and for La Roche between 1923 and 1925.[4] Beginning in the square outside the houses (figs. 47–50), the photographs then draw the reader along the walkway (fig. 51) into the tall central hall of La Roche's house, its staircase and a dazzling, cubic parapet beckoning in the distance (fig. 52). The bold, cantilevered staircase (fig. 53), the bridge across the hall (fig. 54), and the outlook onto it from the dining room (fig. 55) follow, revealing other views of the central void and the large glass wall (*pan de verre*) that illuminates the core of the building. Two skewed shots of the living room, or salon, in fact a picture gallery for La Roche's collection (figs. 56, 57), take up again the act of ascending, emphasized by an anticipatory view of the roof garden through the windows. Finally the terrace is achieved, a planted and furnished space shown from two angles (figs. 58, 59), with a framed vista on the neighboring properties, recalling the unglazed openings that had first attracted the student traveler at the monastery of Galluzzo a decade and a half before. Instead of retracing his steps to complete the visual promenade, Le Corbusier takes us across the shared roof garden and down into the adjoining house to leave us in the Jeannerets' sparsely furnished living room (fig. 60). The photographs emphasize the smooth, unbroken surfaces of the walls, the angles of the staircase, the sweep of the ramp, and the tension between solids and voids, playing down the household furnishings so that little detracts from the impact of his vision. Clearly, he shows us, it is the light filling the interior, creating deep shadows and accentuating the geometry of his broad forms, that brings poetry to the building.

51
52
53

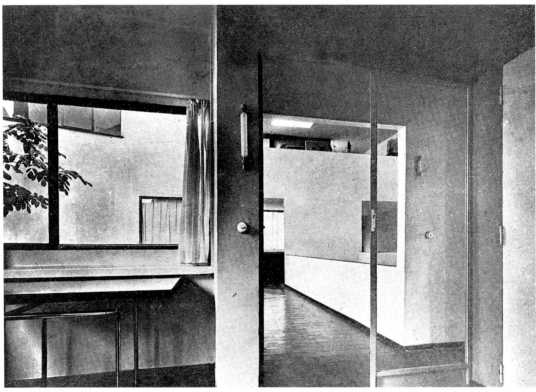

54
55

54 Villa La Roche. Mezzanine, with library above. **55** Villa La Roche. Dining room, with library beyond. **56** Villa La Roche. View from the gallery to roof garden. **57** Villa La Roche. View from the library into salon, or gallery.

56

57

58

59

60

61 Villa La Roche. Central hall. **62** Villa Savoye, Poissy, 1929–31.

58 59

61

62

Because of the large expanses of glass stretching from wall to wall, made possible by the use of reinforced-concrete construction, light could now enter a building in sufficient intensity to illuminate a deep space such as La Roche's central hall (fig. 61). "The room is full of light because the *walls are bright*," Le Corbusier wrote in a series of notes on architecture published in *Cahiers d'Art* in 1926. "The eye no longer sees the walls in shadow and half light. Our feelings are transported, our spirit is transported; we have sun in the room; *it is bright in our house.* . . . We have conquered with technology *the primordial basis of the architectural sensation: light.*"[5] Light may have dominated Le Corbusier's concept of architecture, but the promenade that revealed the architect's eloquent vision through the dimensions of space and time was also enhanced by color, as it was in the contemporaneous Esprit Nouveau pavilion. The commitment to color was not without its dangers, however, as he and Ozenfant had explained in their article on Purism in 1921: "In the expression of volume color is a perilous agent; often it destroys or disorganizes volume because the intrinsic properties of color are very different, some being radiant and pushing forward, others receding, still others being massive and staying in the real plane of the canvas."[6] For Le Corbusier, the use of color in building was "dictated by the luminosity of the wall. And according to the great universal rules: warm tones in the light, cold tones in the shade, I have tried counterpoints and fugues and thus have brought life to the interior situation of the house by trying to follow the modulations of light with color."[7]

A promenade today along the path from the entrance to the rooftop retreat of the restored Villa Savoye in Poissy (fig. 62), the most iconic of the private houses he designed, can provide some understanding of how Le Corbusier expected color and light to have been experienced together. The utilitarian ground floor, with its semicircular glass wall allowing in a muted half light, is neutral, a place of passage (figs. 63, 64), like the white central hall of the Villa La Roche. Its walls and ceramic floor tiles, and the sink placed out in the open, are white; the flooring of the ramp opposite the entrance and of the corkscrew staircase (a stunning sculptural device and a secondary access), doors, built-in tables, and metal handrails are black; the baseboards are gray, completing a Whistlerian environment. This conceit appears to continue as one ascends the ramp, where light first begins to play directly through the triangular opening, and at the switchback, with the gray wall above (fig. 65). There is little to suggest that coloristic effects will greet us when we reach the main floor. But there, views of a hall (fig. 66) or through a doorway into the bedrooms (fig. 67) reveal contrasts of blues, umbers, siennas, and salmon pinks like those in Le Corbusier's description of the Esprit Nouveau pavilion. The doorway in the gray wall (fig. 68) leads to the long living-dining room, the brightest interior space; its far wall is pink, the inner wall is blue, and its floor is yellow tile. Black rims the built-in shelves under the windows, the radiator, fireplace, and cabinets and their silvery metal doors (fig. 69), and the built-in table at the opposite end of the room, with its artfully placed single leg (fig. 70), establishing a unifying horizontal element across the space.

63 Villa Savoye. Entrance hall with ramp and circular staircase. **64** Villa Savoye. Entrance hall.

63

67 68

69 70

Continuing the promenade out through the sliding door of the living room and onto a large enclosed terrace (fig. 71) with walls pierced by both windows and unglazed openings that extend the line of fenestration across the entire building, the multicolored core of the house is left to return to an architecturally neutral environment. Here, the architect has handed back to sunlight and to nature (revealed in the planters and through the viewing apertures) the role of orchestrating light and color. Another ramp is ascended to reach the uppermost level, where a semicircular nook, and, on axis beneath a framed opening, a concrete table firmly wedded to the building, are insistent statements of Le Corbusier's commitment to extending the amenities of his interiors into livable spaces outside (fig. 72). Except for the lack of a roof, little distinguishes the conception of his exterior spaces from that of his open-plan interiors, as is shown in his many sketches of terraces (fig. 73), where inevitably a table is set for tea, or an open book or newspaper awaits the return of a reader. His use of the outdoors reaches perfection at the Villa Savoye, but his attempts to re-create the experience of the walled garden at the monastery of Galluzzo, where health, nature, beauty, harmony, and peace reside, can be seen in even in his earliest architectural drawings (fig. 74).

71

72

73

74

75

75 Villa la Roche. Handrail. **76** Le Corbusier. *Still Life with Numerous Objects*, 1923. Oil on canvas. Fondation Le Corbusier, Paris (175). **77** Color study for the dressing room of the Villa Berque, Paris, 1921–22. Colored chalk and pencil. Fondation Le Corbusier, Paris (9.328).

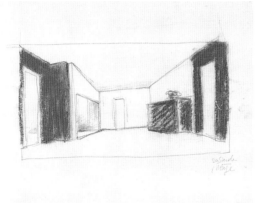

76
77

The colors we see today in Le Corbusier's buildings can only be approximations of the originals, changed over the decades by the architect's reconsiderations, by repainting as needed, by deterioriation through neglect, and then by restoration, sometimes on the basis of incomplete or inconclusive evidence.[8] Archival sources confirm the colors that were originally chosen, even if descriptions of colors are anything but exact. In 1925, for example, the commercial painter A. Célio provided a list of the colors he used to paint the La Roche and Jeanneret houses in Auteuil in distemper and oil: yellow ocher, red ocher, ivory black, raw sienna, burnt sienna, raw umber, burnt umber, English green (fig. 75), ultramarine blue, *bleu charron* (wheelwright blue), and chrome yellow.[9] This duplicates the "major" scale of colors from the Purist palette described in the the article on Purism that Ozenfant and Le Corbusier published in *L'Esprit Nouveau* in 1921, and repeated so definitively in Le Corbusier's intense *Still Life with Numerous Objects* of 1923 (fig. 76). The "major" scale, their article explained, consisted of "ochre yellows, reds, earths, white, black, ultramarine

blue, and, of course, certain of their derivatives; this scale is a strong, stable scale giving unity and holding the plane of the picture since these colors keep one another in balance. They are thus essentially constructive colors; it is these that all the great periods employed; it is these that whoever wishes to paint in volume should use."[10] Visual documentation for the introduction of color into his buildings can be found in Le Corbusier's color notations for several of his buildings; in his colored sketches, from as early as his renovations of the Villa Berque in 1921–22 (fig. 77); and in colored photographic and axonometric illustrations that were published in *Architecture Vivante*. They show how widely color was used, its variety, and its intensity; for example, the deep red and brown walls of the Villa Berque, the Villa Church (with similarly painted window surrounds; fig. 78), and the Villa Cook (fig. 79). The coloristic effect of the liberal application of dark brown and black on such elements as fireplaces and built-in shelves and ledges cannot be conveyed in black and white photographs (compare fig. 79 and fig. 80).

78 Sketch of the living room of the Villa Church, Ville d'Avray, 1928. Pencil and pastel. Fondation Le Corbusier, Paris (8.075). **79** Axonometric drawing of the living room of the Villa Cook, Boulogne-sur-Seine, 1926. From *L'Architecture Vivante* (1927). **80** Villa Cook. Living room. Fondation Le Corbusier, Paris.

In 1931 Le Corbusier and the Swiss Salubra company issued a series of solid-color wallpapers that were meant to standardize the application of color in buildings; and with their Colour Keyboards, the calculated arrangement of samples and templates for viewing them, he tried to make the selection of colors foolproof (fig. 81). The introductory page in the sample book announced Le Corbusier's intentions:

> Salubra is oil paint sold in rolls.
>
> Instead of covering walls and ceilings with "three coats of oils" . . . we can now utilize this "machine-prepared-painting"; and we can apply it at the very last moment of finishing. . . .
>
> The architect is always more or less at the mercy of indifferent workmanship in the matter of painting. The use of Salubra gives him peace of mind; for its proportions of oil and colour are always accurate. Its consistent quality of tone and material is guaranteed. . . .
>
> All of us, according to our taste and reactions, favour one or more dominating schemes of colour. Each individual is drawn towards some particular harmony which seems to accord with his inner feelings. The practical difficulty is to show colours in such a way that the individual can detect his own "affinity."
>
> And that is why the Colour Keyboards have been invented. They show 43 different shades; and I think that even a greater number than this is conceivable. In the making of this present selection, however, I have confined myself within architectural limits, after taking the precaution to ascertain that my own personal taste was in key with the taste of the average healthy individual who, since the world began, and regardless of questions of race or culture, has always utilized colour as a means of expressing his joy in life. . . .
>
> This collection comprises strictly "architectural" shades, of pronounced value for mural effect, and of proved quality; these are the horizontal strips on the various plates. Their function is so important that I have christened each one of these coloured "backgrounds" with a title descriptive of its significance in mural effect, such as "space," "sky," "velvet," "masonry," "sand.". . .
>
> These "Keyboards of Colour" aim at stimulating personal selection, by placing the task of choosing on a sound systematic basis. In my opinion they offer a method of approach which is accurate and effective, one which makes it possible to plan, in the modern home, colour harmonies which are definitely architectural and yet suited to the natural taste and needs of the individual.[11]

78

79

80

81

In his introductory essay on architectural polychromy prepared for the catalog but never published with it, he used examples of his own work to demonstrate just what color could do. It could be employed, he explained, to modify space or the impression of the form of an interior or an object, that is, to "camouflage" it, or to "establish a hierarchy, to play down defects or bothersome but inevitable complexities; to attract the eye to the essential, to what can give the sensation of purity, to reveal pure form."[12] In choosing the Jeanneret living room as an example (fig. 82), he explicated his strategy for using polychromy to make a room seem less narrow:

> Let us look for a subterfuge…let us create space by a useful contrast of colors and through their clever arrangement. The basis will be white; but we will paint two of the walls pale pink (light burnt Sienna), another wall opposite, *pale green*; the rest white, the ceiling white. Illusion is born; the walls are no longer exactly opposite; the eye skips from a pink surface to a green surface, to other white ones; the form of the room retreats.
>
> In this small living room, we had built from cement blocks a chimney and cabinets at heights of 75 and 90 centimeters; these elements that add to our comfort form a spine that juts into the room and creates architectural volumes that are somewhat too encumbering. In addition, the stack from the fireplace joined with that from the central heating form a round pipe in the open.
>
> Color *can destroy the uniformity of volume*. The chimney pipe is painted white. It is connected with the white ceiling; it merges into it. It no longer catches the eye, except in its luminous aspect as a bright cylinder, with the purity of its light tone. The fireplace and the cabinets are painted pure burnt Sienna, which is dark and absorbs light; the confusing volumes are unified. This long dark mass, contrasting strongly to the bright walls and pale ceiling, ceases to belong to the room architecturally. It has become a fitting, like a piece of furniture. It is independent, it no longer encumbers; color has conferred on it a new aspect.[13]

In contrast, color could also be used to unify a room, and to give it a special ambience, as was done with Raoul La Roche's conventional, rectangular dining room. Le Corbusier painted all four of the walls, as well as the ceiling, salmon pink (fig. 83), which seems to deviate from this theory of receding and advancing colors, but he explained its rationale:

> If the four walls are all painted the same tone, the form of the room remains intact; it is very assertive if the tones "hold the wall" (reds for example), very subdued if the tones break the wall (blues for example). The form of the room will be totally maintained, revealed, if the ceiling is painted white.
>
> If the ceiling is of the same tone as the wall, the impression is totally modified; from something distinct one moves to something very soft, calm, enchanting, like being under a dome. I have enclosed the space."[14]

Le Corbusier introduced color, as he told it, to reinforce the spatial conception of his buildings, both outside (for example, the green walls that make the Villa Savoye seem to float in its meadow) and inside. But always the artist, he did not consistently apply color in strict accordance with his theories of receding and advancing, soothing and exciting colors. Nor would he always be able to control the experience of light and color as he might have liked. His theory of warm tones in light, cold tones in shade falls apart in the face of differing sources and luminosities of light, as when the direction and angle of light entering a room change throughout the day (and when a room has several exposures) or when days are bright or dull. Nor does his theory account for the changing tones and values of white itself under similar circumstances, or for the unavoidable spill-over from a wall of one color to a wall of another, particularly when the adjacent wall is painted white. Moreover, not all of Le Corbusier's clients were willing to go along with his desire for colored walls, as we learn from a letter from his expatriate American client Henry Church: "In the interior," Church wrote to Le Corbusier about the renovations of his house in Ville d'Avray in 1928, "I want neither blue nor

82
83

84

umber. Please let me know if you have something else to suggest. Otherwise, we propose, with your agreement, to start from the proposition that the second building will be painted white inside and out, at any rate unless by common agreement we decide on other colours."[15]

As much as daylight, supported by color, energized Le Corbusier, artifical light dismayed him. "Modern artifical light is intense, sharp,"[16] he complained in his notes on architecture in *Cahiers d'Art* in 1926, and like most designers of his day, he was undecided about how best to exploit this medium in modern domestic environments. "Headlights, reflectors, spotlights on the ceiling, or on the ground, or vertical within the embrasures of the windows or at the corner of rooms. We blunder with the stammerings of a totally new invention. We rarely, very rarely, occupy ourselves with this question.... I tried to light two houses in Auteuil without any lamps in the ceiling; it is not conclusive."[17] Le Corbusier, in fact, had great trouble with lighting at the Auteuil houses, and it was not resolved for years, the initial systems being provisional as he indicated. These early interiors were the proving grounds, where his conceptions and their practicalities were tested. In August 1925, soon after the house was occupied, La Roche wrote to apprise the architect of the situation in the living room, where strip lights had been placed in the channel at the base of the windows: "This gives quite a pleasant light, but evidently not very bright. Even when all seven lamps are on, you can barely see to read."[18] Later, after an absence, La Roche found "the dining room ceiling full of holes. I had hoped that you were going to carry out the scheme of ceiling lights (provisional system) which we had discussed. I understand perfectly your hesitancy over the way to light my house. But until you find something really good, it is essential at least that I should be able to see clearly in my home. It's six months since I moved in and I am still obliged to use illumination which, particularly in the painting gallery, relies on ad hoc arrangements.... I come back to the point that a perfectly banal system would be the best solution, or at least for the moment [fig. 84]."[19] By the following January a temporary system had been installed in the gallery, strings of light bulbs running across the space, seen in early photographs (fig. 85), but this too was makeshift. When the gallery had to be renovated after pipes in the wall burst there in 1928, a completely new arrangement for lighting was installed, a single bulb at the end of a long pole jutting out from the wall above the door at the foot of the ramp (fig. 86) and a long blue-metal trough

86 Villa La Roche. Gallery with bulb on pole at foot of ramp. **87** Drawings for light trough in the Villa La Roche gallery, 1928. Pencil. Fondation Le Corbusier, Paris (15.284). **88** Light trough in the gallery of the Villa La Roche. **89** Villa Savoye. Living room, c. 1930. Fondation Le Corbusier, Paris.

86

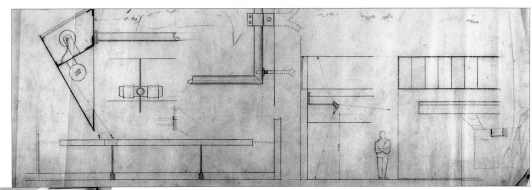

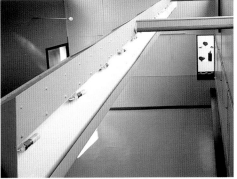

87
88
89

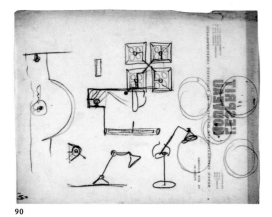
90

enclosing a row of bulbs, which extended the length of the opposite wall at the base of the windows (figs. 87, 88). The long, shiny metal fixture that runs the length of the living room of the Villa Savoye (fig. 89), which was under construction at the same time as the renovations at the Villa La Roche, has a certain resemblance to the Auteuil light trough, but its origin is different; it duplicated one encountered by Mme Savoy on a visit to a refrigeration showroom, which she recommended to the architects.

Le Corbusier decidedly avoided giving consideration to lamps as objects beyond their function: a bare bulb, whatever its shape or intensity, was sufficient unless its glare required a reflector of some sort, or if it needed mobility (fig. 90). The firm of Marc Chalier in Paris made many of his fixtures during the 1920s, the most resolved being the applique with an exposed lighting tube held top and bottom by a simple bracket (fig. 91), which was used in the Auteuil houses and in the Esprit Nouveau pavilion. A fixture such as this with its exposed bulb was unusual then, and was appreciated by Georges Draeger of the respected French printing firm Draeger Frères, who wrote to the architect asking if he could have sketches of the different fixtures Le Corbusier used, wishing to replace the "vulgar commercial models in my office, which I put there temporarily" (fig. 92).

In fitting out the private houses with cabinets and other storage elements, Le Corbusier generally ignored the standard modular system he had created for the Esprit Nouveau pavilion. He chose instead to design built-in units adapted to the particularities and peculiarities of their bedrooms, libraries, hallways, and kitchens (although regular freestanding units were sometimes used to form internal partitions as they had in the exhibition houses in Paris and

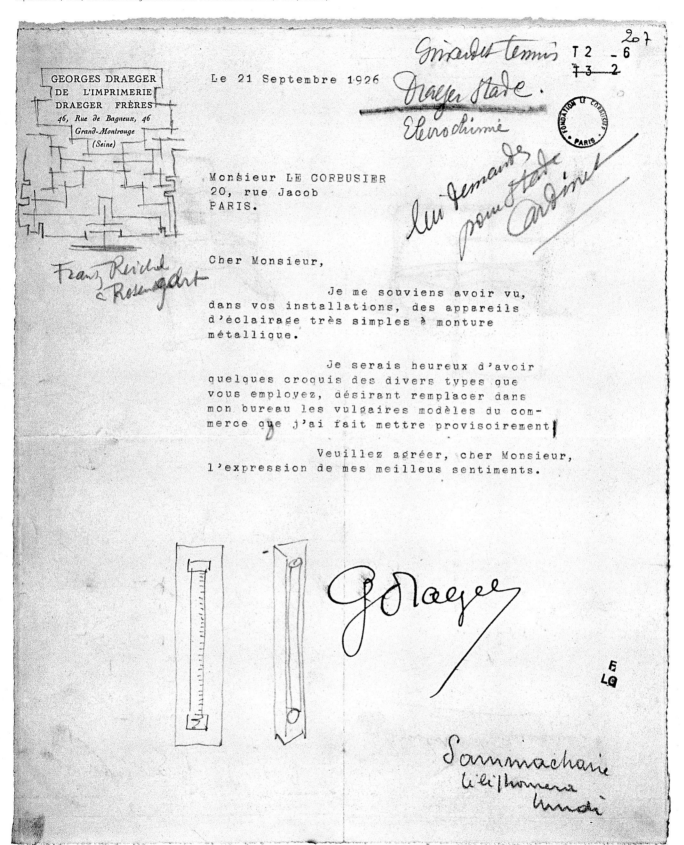

GEORGES DRAEGER
DE L'IMPRIMERIE
DRAEGER FRÈRES
46, Rue de Bagneux, 46
Grand-Montrouge
(Seine)

Le 21 Septembre 1926

Monsieur LE CORBUSIER
20, rue Jacob
PARIS.

Cher Monsieur,

Je me souviens avoir vu, dans vos installations, des appareils d'éclairage très simples à monture métallique.

Je serais heureux d'avoir quelques croquis des divers types que vous employez, désirant remplacer dans mon bureau les vulgaires modèles du commerce que j'ai fait mettre provisoirement

Veuillez agréer, cher Monsieur, l'expression de mes meilleus sentiments.

91 92

93 Drawing for kitchen cabinets of the Villa Savoye, 1929. Pencil and ink. Fondation Le Corbusier, Paris (19.464). 94 Villa Savoye. Cabinets and pass-through dividing kitchen and pantry. 95 Villa La Roche. Library with bookshelves integrated with wall of parapet. 96 Drawing for the living room fireplace, Villa Savoye. Pencil. Fondation Le Corbusier, Paris (19.518). 97 Drawing for a table between two cabinets, Villa Savoye. Pencil. Fondation Le Corbusier, Paris (19.524).

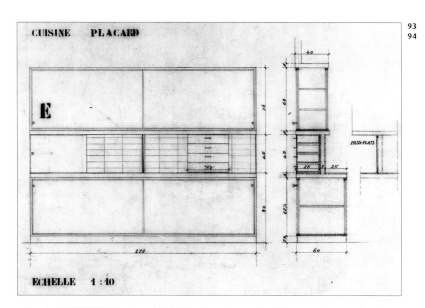

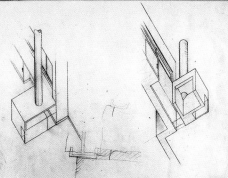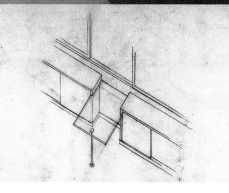

Stuttgart). While he had particularized the interiors of his modular units to accommodate their diverse contents, Le Corbusier generalized the interiors of most of these cabinets. The tiled kitchen of the Villa Savoye, for example, has cupboards with oversize metal sliding doors and long, widely spaced shelves, but nothing in his drawings or in the built work gives any consideration to accommodating the specific types and sizes of objects that were to be contained within (figs. 93, 94). Le Corbusier frequently took advantage of windows, radiators, and parapets as readymade elements that offered or demanded shelving and ledges (fig. 95). These were generally continuations of the concrete structure of the building, and often integrated the freestanding fireplaces that were built in many of his living rooms (fig. 96). Corners and columns also offered support for tables and ledges, and the presence of any unusual structural event was an invitation to bridge a gap or integrate several fittings into a more harmonious totality (fig. 97).

The British scholar Tim Benton, who worked assiduously to bring order to the study of Le Corbusier's houses, has written of their "poignant" detailing and "touchingly sincere craftsmanship," pointing out as examples the small drainage holes beneath the windows to catch condensation and the channels devised to carry it away (fig. 98), the door and cupboard handles and latches (fig. 99), and the placement of lights and skylights.[20] While Le Corbusier took a great deal of care with such small architectural details of his houses, he seems to have been considerably less concerned about the freestanding furniture that would fill them. He indicated furniture in the presentation drawings made to show his clients how their houses would look, most often simply repeating ideograms of generic forms such as those used in the Esprit Nouveau pavilion. For most of the houses, commercial selection following the concept of the pavilion was allowed to determine the furniture, with bentwood chairs by Thonet and club chairs by Maple

98 Villa La Roche. Drainage hole under window. 99 Drawing of door handles and a lock for the Villa Les Terraces (Stein–de Monzie), Garches, 1927. Pencil, colored pencil, and ink. Fondation Le Corbusier, Paris (10.542). 100 Villa Les Terraces. Entrance and hall. Fondation Le Corbusier, Paris.

98
99

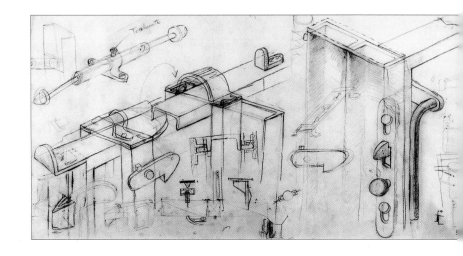

100

used primarily (major exceptions were the Steins, who came with antiques, and, of course, the Ternisiens, who came with bric-a-brac). For the photographs in his books and articles, however, he preferred architecture to dwellings, often illustrating bare interiors taken before his clients had moved in, especially when he was not completely responsible for their furnishings (fig. 100). Yet he also felt he had to demonstrate that his buildings could be inhabited, and he would create suggestive vignettes to add poetic meaning through their photographic representation—combining furniture, built-ins, and personal objects (such as his coat and hat) to suggest the welcoming presence of the architect in his buildings (fig. 101), or other groupings that spoke jointly of symbol, sentiment, and type, such as a half loaf of bread, a glass, and a coffeepot on a kitchen counter (fig. 102). These symbols and allusions were meant to say that the buildings, however modern and spare they might seem, should still be thought of as home.

Le Corbusier had generally left the details of completing the firm's buildings under the supervision of Pierre Jeanneret, but responsibility for the interiors and furnishings was taken on in fall 1927 by Charlotte Perriand, the young associate who was hired for that purpose. Their first meeting, when this attractive and electric young woman, under the spell of Le Corbusier's writings, presented herself at the studio to ask for work, had not gone well, as she recalled:

> One afternoon, a portfolio of drawings under my arm, somewhat intimidated by the austerity of the premises, I found myself face to face with Le Corbusier's large eyeglasses, which concealed his gaze. His greeting was rather cold and distant. "What do you want?" "To work with you." He glanced quickly through my drawings. "We don't embroider cushions here," was his response. He led me to the door. In a final attempt I left my address and told him about my installation at the Salon d'Automne—without any hope that he would see it. I went away feeling almost relieved. No one could say that my charm had worked on him.[21]

But this condescending attitude changed the very next morning when Le Corbusier and Jeanneret visited the Salon d'Automne and saw Perriand's striking metal "Bar sous le toit" ("Bar in the Attic") installation, deciding on the spot to hire her. A tight, intimate space with pastel walls and sleek chromed-steel and aluminum bar, stools, and tables, the "Bar sous le toit" was made of the most modern of materials (see fig. 118). Although she had exhibited furnishings at earlier salons, this was her first foray into the new, progressive design of metal.

For Perriand it was a privilege to work in Le Corbusier's architectural office, housed in an old convent on the rue de Sèvres on the Left Bank, where Pierre Jeanneret kept things running, following up on the drawings and details for each project and overseeing the young architects who had made the pilgrimage to Paris to work for the master, already known worldwide through his writings. Her initial project was at the Villa La Roche, where renovations were begun early in 1928, and her first visit to the house in Auteuil in Le Corbusier's company overwhelmed her. "What a shock it was," she recalled, "to enter this space bathed in cantatas

101
102

101 Villa Savoye. Entrance hall. Fondation Le Corbusier, Paris. **102** Villa Savoye. Kitchen. Fondation Le Corbusier, Paris. **103** Color study for the remodeling of the gallery of the Villa La Roche, 1928. Pencil, ink, and gouache. Fondation Le Corbusier, Paris (15.251). **104** Drawing for remodeling of the gallery of the Villa La Roche, 1928. Pencil. Fondation Le Corbusier, Paris (15.290).

of Johann Sebastian Bach (Corbu had plugged in the gramophone). It was like religiously stepping into an unknown musical, harmonious world, to find oneself by osmosis in total communion with the whole. . . . Le Corbusier truly had me."[22]

The renovations in La Roche's gallery (figs. 103, 104) were all inclusive. They comprised the lighting (see figs. 86–88); storage cabinets that replaced a wall and cupboard under the ramp and included a small inset mirror, which created a curious spatial illusion of doubly curving walls (fig. 105); marble table in the center of the room (fig. 106); a revision of the painting program with walls of gray, yellow, brown, and white, and gray trim; and the replacement of the floor with pink rubber carpeting and the ramp with gray.[23] Here for the first time in the firm's buildings, luxurious materials and nods to stylish living were introduced, very likely the result of Perriand's enthusiasm. This is most apparent in the gleaming black marble-top table, which she may have designed. At one end it rests on a stand of thick tubular steel welded into a V, at the other, on a support covered with large black-glazed ceramic tiles matching the long rectangle in the floor on which the table sits.

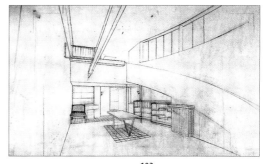

103
104

This bold but somewhat gratuitous decorative addition, an anomaly in a house that had in many ways been conceived as an austere, monastic dwelling (fig. 107), anticipates the luxurious, customized built-in features that began to appear in the firm's other houses at the time. Most impressive is the splendid skylit sunken bath installed in the Villa Savoye, separated from the master bedroom by a curtain (figs. 108, 109). It is decoratively lined with variegated blue tiles, while a built-in undulating chaise longue, faced with gray tile and edged in black tile, sits at its end. In its zigzag form and its stylish luxury, the tiled chaise anticipates the tubular-metal chaise longue that was then in the design stage under Perriand's direction, its shape being worked out along with those of the cushioned club chair and armchair with pivoting back. It was in La Roche's renovated gallery that the three completed metal furniture designs seem to have been first photographed, brought together around the marble table, which again in a symbolic gesture was set with a convivial tray with liquor, glasses, and a coffee cup, and displayed the architect's gloves hanging over the side (fig. 110). This obviously was a publicity shot, perhaps taken just in time for publication in the first volume of Le Corbusier and Jeanneret's complete works, which was issued in 1929.[24] The chairs did not then belong to La Roche (although later he bought both armchairs), and he probably did not even know that the photograph was being taken, for Le Corbusier seems to have had the run of the house. A suite of the metal designs was also made for the Villa Church and photographed there, and similarly reproduced in the *Oeuvre complète*. These included two armchairs with pivoting backs, a large-size stuffed club chair, and a chaise longue, all made to furnish its library in a modern fashion (figs. 111, 112; shown with the architect's hat and gloves and open books, again a sentimental touch). In addition, Perriand noted, "built-in storage units, and tables, including one made of a large block of unpolished glass in a wonderful 'golden' color—a magnificent glassmaker's product by Saint-Gobain"[25] were created. The

golden glass table with metal base was used in the library, while another glass table was made for the dining room, and armchairs with revolving backs and matching stools, which Perriand herself had designed and shown first in the 1928 spring Salon des Artistes Décorateurs, accompanied it (fig. 113). These startlingly new furniture designs in metal were brought from initial conception through various prototype stages to final models between 1927 and 1928 under the watchful eye of Perriand alongside other interior work she was overseeing. Additional examples were made for clients over the next year, but they were not unveiled to the public until 1929, when they were shown at the Salon d'Automne of 1929, shown there in an installation called the "Interior Equipment of a Dwelling."

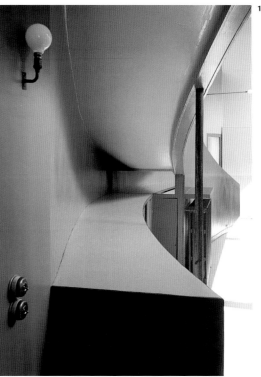

105

106
107

NOTES

1. For information on the individual houses, see Tim Benton, *The Villas of Le Corbusier, 1920–1930* (New Haven, Conn.: Yale University Press, 1987).
2. Raoul La Roche to Le Corbusier, May 24, 1926; trans. in ibid., 70.
3. Trans. in ibid., 100.
4. Le Corbusier, *Almanach d'architecture moderne* (Paris: Les Editions G. Crès et Cie, 1926), 41–54.
5. Le Corbusier, "Notes à la suite," *Cahiers d'Art* 3 (1926): 46–48.
6. Amédée Ozenfant and Ch.-E. Jeanneret, "Le Purisme," *L'Esprit Nouveau* 4 (1921): 369–86; trans. in *Modern Artists on Art: Ten Unabridged Essays*, ed. Robert L. Herbert (Englewood Cliffs, N.J.: Prentice-Hall, 1964), 70.
7. "Notes à la Suite," op. cit., 48.
8. See Guillemette Moret-Journel, *The Savoy House, Poissy-Yvelines* (Paris: Editions du Patrimoine, 1998), 9–10.
9. A. Célio to Jeanneret, March 12, 1925, FLC H1-3-254.
10. Trans. in Herbert, op. cit., 70.
11. Le Corbusier, "Colour Keyboards," introduction to the first Salubra collection; reprinted in *Polychromie Architecturale: Le Corbusier's Color Keyboards from 1931 and 1959*, ed. Arthur Rüegg (Basel, Boston, and Berlin: Birkhäuser, 1997), 150–51.
12. Le Corbusier, "Architectural Polychromy," in ibid., 121 [translation modified].
13. Ibid., 123, 125 [translation modified].
14. Ibid., 119 [translation modified].
15. Henry Church to Le Corbusier, July 9, 1928; trans. in Benton, op. cit., 109.
16. "Notes à la suite," op. cit., 46.
17. Ibid., 49.
18. Raoul La Roche to Le Corbusier, August 16, 1925; trans. in Benton, op. cit., 65.
19. Raoul La Roche to Le Corbusier, October 1925; trans. in ibid., 65.
20. Ibid., 28.
21. Charlotte Perriand, *Une Vie de création* (Paris: Editions Odile Jacob, 1998), 25.
22. Ibid., 28.
23. Benton, op. cit., 72, describes these later additions to the gallery.
24. *Le Corbusier et Pierre Jeanneret: Oeuvre complète de 1910–1929*, ed. W. Boesiger and O. Stonorov, 4th ed. (Zurich: Les Editions d'Architecture Erlenbach, 1946), 157. A second version of this shot is illustrated in Francis Jourdain, *Intérieures* (Paris: n.p., n.d.), pl. 17.
25. Perriand, op. cit., 34.

110 112
111 113

110 Villa La Roche. Gallery with the firm's metal furniture, c. 1929. Fondation Le Corbusier, Paris. **111** Villa Church. Library with the firm's metal furniture, c. 1929. Fondation Le Corbusier, Paris.
112 Villa Church. Library with the firm's metal furniture, c. 1929. Fondation Le Corbusier, Paris. **113** Villa Church. Dining room with the firm's metal furniture, c. 1929. Fondation Le Corbusier, Paris.

5

The Furniture of Le Corbusier,
Jeanneret, and Perriand

interior equipment of a dwelling

Le Corbusier does not seem to have used the term *equipment* to refer to the firm's new metal furniture much before May 1929, when he wrote to M. Bonifay, secretary of the Salon d'Automne, advising him that they "would like to participate in the next Salon with an *important entry: the equipment of a modern apartment.*"[1] It would be there that the furniture designs photographed at the Villa La Roche and the Villa Church would first be fully presented to the public (fig. 114). The use of the collective "equipment" signaled a new approach on the part of Le Corbusier; previously he had considered utilitarian objects as discrete implements, or tools, extensions of the body, with each individually adapted to its specific use. It was this viewpoint that had supported his earlier attitude to furnishing, exemplified by the selection and assemblage of disparate, and what he thought were timeless, objects in the Esprit Nouveau pavilion in 1925. He chose each independently for its type and without regard for uniformity, asking whether the "rational perfection and precise formulation in each does not constitute sufficient common ground between them to allow the recognition of a *style*!"[2] Late in the decade, however, he broadened his approach and began to view type objects in a collective context as "equipment," referring specifically to the furniture recently created by the firm. "The term furniture contains for me something vague, disorderly, and a multitude of senseless trash," he wrote somewhat later, "whereas in the contrary the conception of equipment means utility and real and exact functions. It saves time, labour and money. In one word, an end to senseless expenditure. I unite in the term equipment all the functions of daily life. . . . In older times, tools with all their shortcomings; today, equipment with all its advantages."[3] It is ironic that Le Corbusier chose to adopt this industrial term to describe the new metal furniture, works that could in no way be considered merely utilitarian in their formulation. However much they responded to Le Corbusier's ideas of type use, and however mechanistic their fabrication in tubular metal was thought to be, they were neither standardized nor economical nor designed for efficient mass production. Above all, this "equipment" was an exercise in luxury and style, a challenge for primacy in modern design thrown down in response to a fad initiated in Germany a few years earlier when modern furniture made of metal was first introduced there.

This emphasis on style and on a unified design aesthetic, which would also characterize the firm's Salon installation, may in part be linked to Charlotte Perriand's arrival, and it was mirrored in the distinctive maquette created in advance of the exhibition for publication in *Architecture Vivante* early in 1930 (fig. 115). Instead of the plans, axonometric drawings, and photographs that had documented Le Corbusier's previous work, the magazine reproduced this modernist color montage, which brought an up-to-date graphic vocabulary to the presentation of the "important" modern apartment. Among the various pieces of furniture and the line of cabinets shown in somewhat contradictory scale and perspective is a curious shot of Charlotte Perriand reclining in the chaise longue, head averted. This picture is similar to one that accompanied her article "Wood or Metal?" in *The Studio* in March 1929 (fig. 116), her response to English critic John Gloag's gloomy assessment of the "utter inhumanity" of metal furniture in his article of the same name published earlier in the year.[4] Adopting a prose style dependent on Le Corbusier's own polemical writings, Perriand announced that "METAL plays the same part in furniture as cement has done in architecture. *IT IS A REVOLUTION*," and summarized for *Studio* readers what she thought was the aesthetic impact that modern materials could have:

> If we use metal in conjunction with
> leather for chairs, with marble slabs, glass
> and india-rubber for tables, floor coverings,
> cement,
> vegetable substances,
> we get a range of wonderful combinations
> and new aesthetic effects.
> UNITY IN ARCHITECTURE and yet
> again
> POETRY
> A new lyric beauty, regenerated by
> mathematical science.[5]

In creating their metal furniture, apparently published for the first time in the context of the *Studio* article, the firm was staking out its own territory, and attempting to create a forceful French presence, in the burgeoning battle of furniture made of metal. This worldwide interest in metal was being dominated by a number of well-respected modernist designers in Germany, notably Marcel Breuer (who started it all in 1925 with his tubular-steel armchair), and the firm's public foray into metal was late in the game for this short-lived craze. A large representation of metal designs in many different configurations and styles had been produced by architects and designers all over Europe, including France, during the previous four years and shown at housing and furnishings exhibitions; even in Japan, as early as 1928, examples of Western-style tubular metal furniture had begun to be manufactured, their frames, fabrication methods, and upholstery carefully studied and then directly

114 "Interior Equipment of a Dwelling" installation at the Salon d'Automne, Paris, 1929. Fondation Le Corbusier, Paris. **115** Montage representing the Salon d'Automne installation. From *Architecture Vivante* (1930).

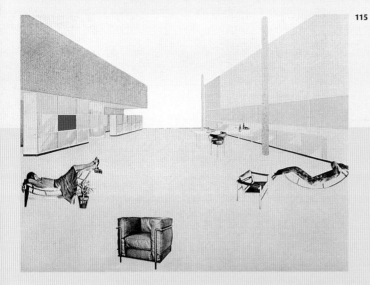

115

114

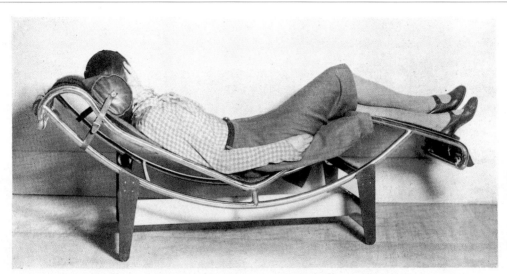

Metal Couch designed by Le Corbusier, Pierre Jeanneret and Charlotte Perriand

WOOD OR METAL?

A reply to Mr. John Gloag's article in our January issue by Charlotte Perriand who, as champion of new ideas, has adopted an original style of expressing them

METAL plays the same part in furniture as cement has done in architecture.

IT IS A REVOLUTION.

The FUTURE will favour materials which best solve the problems propounded by the new man :

I understand by the NEW MAN the type of individual who keeps pace with scientific thought, who understands his age and lives it : The Aeroplane, the Ocean Liner and the Motor are at his service ;

Sport gives him health ;

His House is his resting place.

WHAT IS HIS HOUSE TO BE?

Hygiene must be considered first : soap and water.

Tidiness : standard cupboards with partitions for these.

Rest · resting machines for ease and pleasant repose.

Beds : armchairs : chaises longues :

Office chairs and tables : Stools, some high and some low : Folding chairs.

The French word for furniture, " MEUBLES " comes from the Latin " mobilis " : meaning things that can be moved about.

The only things that come into this category are chairs and tables.

We have stated the problem ; now we must solve it. . . .

MATERIAL NOW IN USE AND MATERIAL THAT OUGHT TO BE USED.

WOOD : a vegetable substance, in its very nature bound to decay, it is susceptible to the action of damp in the air. " Central heating dries the air and warps wood." Since the war, we don't get dry wood any more : it is dried by artificial means, and inadequately.

Plywood : Composition wood :

These should be used for panels, mounted on a metal framework, and allowing for " play."

METAL : a homogeneous material of which certain alloys are liable to be affected by acids in the air :

In that case protection is afforded by oxidising, or by application of paint, Duco, etc. . . .

Cupboards of beaten sheet iron :

For chairs, metal " bicycle " tubes :

A bicycle weighs only 10 to 12 kilograms. The minimum of weight, the maximum of strength :

Autogenous welding = △

This process opens a vast field of practical possibilities.

The ratio between the weight necessary to ensure against breakage and the conditions of construction, in other words, the coefficient of security, would be about 6 in the case of metal, 10 in the case of wood. To be of the same solidity the wood would have to be 14 times as thick as metal :

THRUST
COMPRESSION } 14 times more in
FLEXION } wood than in steel

TECHNICAL CONCLUSIONS :

The EIFFEL TOWER could never have been made of Wood.

Metal is superior to wood ; reasons ?

The power of resistance in metal itself ;

Because it allows of mass production in the factory (lessens amount of labour required);

Because by means of the different methods of manufacture it opens out new vistas ; new opportunities of design ;

Because the protective coatings against toxic agencies not only lower the cost of upkeep, but have a considerable ÆSTHETIC value.

METAL plays the same part in furniture as cement has done in architecture.

IT IS A REVOLUTION.

ÆSTHETICS OF METAL.

Aluminium varnish, Duco,

Parkerisation, Paint,

all provide variety in the treatment of metal.

If we use metal in conjunction with leather for chairs, with marble slabs, glass and india-rubber for tables, floor coverings, cement,

vegetable substances,

we get a range of wonderful combinations and new æsthetic effects.

UNITY IN ARCHITECTURE and yet again

POETRY

A new lyric beauty, regenerated by mathematical science ;

Has produced a new kind of man who can love with fervour ; Orly's "Avion Voisin," a photograph of the Mediterranean, and "Ombres Blanches."

Even Mont Cervin is restored to a place of honour.

AS FOR THE PUBLIC :

OPERATION THEATRES :   Clinics, Hospitals :

Improve physical and moral health,

Nothing extraneous.

FASHION : Look at the shops (which serve the public taste).

They make metallised wood ;

They make imitation oak of metal ;

They have even planned a chair made of plywood, metal and india-rubber to imitate marble.

LONG LIVE COMMERCE.

THE MAN OF THE XXth CENTURY :

An INTRUDER ? Yes, he is, when surrounded by antique furniture, and NO, in the setting of the new Interior.

SPORT, *indispensable for a healthy life in a mechanical age.*

Modern mentality also suggests :

Transparency, reds, blues,

The brilliance of coloured paint,

That chairs are for sitting on,

That cupboards are for holding our belongings,

Space, light,

The Joy of creating and of living . . .

in this century of ours.

BRIGHTNESS LOYALTY LIBERTY
          in thinking and acting.

WE MUST KEEP MORALLY AND PHYSICALLY FIT.

Bad luck for those who do not.

CH. PERRIAND.

Comfortable chair, in steel treated with Duco, and leather. By Le Corbusier, Pierre Jeanneret and Charlotte Perriand

117 Interior of one of two houses designed by Le Corbusier and Pierre Jeanneret for the Weissenhof experimental housing exhibition, Stuttgart, 1927. Fondation Le Corbusier, Paris. 118 Charlotte Perriand. "Bar sous le toit" ("Bar in the Attic") installation at the Salon d'Automne, Paris, 1927. 119 Charlotte Perriand. Extendable table and chair with revolving back, 1928. Centre Georges Pompidou, Paris. These were part of the dining room created for the Salon des Artistes Décorateurs, Paris, 1928.

117

copied from German models.[6] Le Corbusier, whose rhetoric in *The Decorative Art of Today* had called for the selection of type objects, not the creation of new ones, must have decided then that he too had to become a significant player in a field that spoke of machine age modernity, even if this meant a departure from "tools" into "style," which would bring him closer to the despised arena of the "decorative arts" than he might have cared to acknowledge.

Le Corbusier had used tubular metal before in a strictly utilitarian fashion for bed frames and table bases, and he had anticipated a notable entrance into the fray two years earlier when the firm was working on the buildings in Stuttgart created for the Weissenhof international housing exhibition. On a preliminary trip to Stuttgart in November 1926, he had been present at a now legendary meeting with Mies van der Rohe and the Dutch architect Mart Stam, at which Stam sketched out his idea for a metal cantilever chair (thereby claiming a modern precedence for the cantilever principle in furniture). By then Le Corbusier must have realized that the other architects represented at Weissenhof would be fitting out their buildings with modern furniture made of this new material and probably felt he had no choice but to compete with them on their terms. By summer 1927, when his Stuttgart buildings were nearing completion, he had already worked on designs for metal furniture, as he informed Alfred Roth, who was the firm's associate at the site overseeing the construction: "For the furniture, we are going to send you in 8 days the drawings of the first armchairs," he wrote. "We are having models in iron tubes executed here. As soon as the models are ready, you will receive the design."[7] But the letter was premature; either the models were not executed or they were not satisfactory, for Roth never received these drawings and he had to fall back on the type furnishings of Le Corbusier's earlier interiors (along with metal beds of his own design) as his inspiration for the Weissenhof furnishings (fig. 117).

The lack of success in creating metal furniture for the Stuttgart exhibition may have convinced Le Corbusier that if he was to produce a competitive line of metal furniture he had to find an associate with experience in furniture and interior design, for soon after, in fall 1927, the firm hired Charlotte Perriand for the job.

There has been much speculation about just how pivotal Perriand was in the design of the tubular-metal pieces, for she was given full responsibility for the fabrication of the metal prototypes and full charge of the manufacture of furniture when she came to the studio, turning this occupation almost into a separate business within the firm. Perriand already had designed metal furniture for her own "Bar sous le toit" installation, the ensemble at the Salon d'Automne of 1927 that had received Le Corbusier's approving eye (fig. 118). Moreover, at the same time as she was struggling with the studio's prototypes, she was also independently preparing a dining room installation for the Salon des Artistes Décorateurs for spring 1928. There she was to exhibit her own furniture made of tubular steel—revolving stool-shaped armchairs upholstered in leather (they have antecedents in the wooden revolving chairs of similar shapes in the catalogs of Thonet) and a telescoping table with U-shaped metal legs (fig. 119). The originality of this installation was generously praised by reviewers[8] and it was illustrated in a number of magazines of furniture and decoration. "The dining room of Charlotte Perriand," the reviewer for *Art et Décoration* mused, "would charm a Brillat Savarin of 1928 with its gaiety, its conveniences so well disposed to the pleasure of the table and of good company."[9] Perriand made a significant distinction, however, between the underlying conception of her own revolving armchair, which had structurally integrated upholstery, and that of the firm's three jointly designed chairs in tubular metal, which were conceived differently, with their upholstery completely independent of the metal skeletons. In her many discussions of these designs, Perriand never suggested that the firm's metal furniture was anything but collaborative, nor did she dispute that the overall formal conception belonged to Le Corbusier. The collaboration was officially corroborated when the patent taken out on the chaise longue was registered jointly in the names of the three associates, while the roles of the three were more clearly spelled out in a letter written by Le Corbusier in 1964 to the Brazilian architect Lucio Costa (with a copy sent to Perriand): "I created with Charlotte Perriand and Pierre Jeanneret (but of my invention), three types of furniture, in 1928, which are considered by public opinion as the most modern to this day."[10]

Perriand was instrumental in refining the designs and working out their details while executing the prototypes in metal, but there can be no doubt that the form and typology of these pieces, that is, their "invention," predate her arrival in the studio of Le Corbusier and Jeanneret in fall 1927. Le Corbusier had already begun to analyze the distinct problems of seating and to classify seating positions by types in a drawing of April 1927 (fig. 120). These may have been connected with plans for his own designs for furniture at that time, possibly for the demonstration housing in Stuttgart. (Similar designs would reemerge in the illustrations for his lectures on furniture presented during 1929 on his trip to South America and published the following year in his book *Précisions*; fig. 121). Chairs that match four of these seating types, classifications that Le Corbusier enumerated in his lectures—relaxation, comfort, conversation, and work (or dining)—are resolved and clearly visualized in sketches for the interior of the Villa Baizeau in the Tunisian

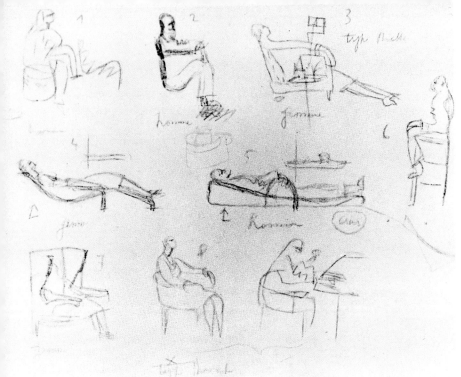
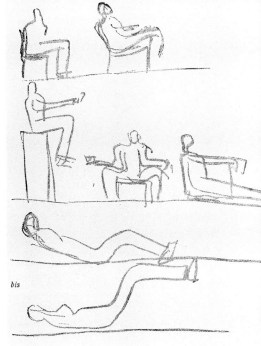

town of Carthage (fig. 122) done early in 1928 before any of the tubular-metal designs had been realized. In drawings of the living room and dining room of the villa, four chairs representing these seating types are laid out across the two sheets almost as a manifesto. From left, in the living room, is a design for complete relaxation, a zigzag lounge form, which rests on the floor at two points and has a single column supporting the head; for comfort, he indicates a Maple-type easy chair shown from behind; and for conversation, a vernacular wooden chair with canvas upholstery, pivoting back, and straps for arms. On the right, for dining, are upright Thonet bentwood office chairs, like those used in the Esprit Nouveau pavilion. But the metal furniture must have been in the works, for soon after, in sketches for the Villa Ocampo in Buenos Aires, made in September of the same year, Le Corbusier would introduce schematics of the new designs corresponding to three of these forms (fig. 123), with the metal chaise longue and club chair shown in the living area and Perriand's revolving armchairs around the table in the dining room. A colored sketch for the Villa Church from spring 1928 (see fig. 78) must be a transitional stage in the furniture-design process; it includes a chaise longue in the zigzag form with supporting column, covered in pony skin and with an adjustable reading stand (not unlike one that Le Corbusier had depicted several years earlier in a drawing of a Morris chair), but also a low chair of tubular metal, an elongated version of what would develop into the armchair with pivoting back. This suggests that metal furniture was very much part of the conception of the renovation at the Villa Church, not a last-minute addition

after the designs were completed. By the middle of the following year, even before the Salon d'Automne exhibition, these pieces had already become ideograms for the firm, as seen, for example, in a project for the Maison Caneel in Brussels (fig. 124).

Overseeing the development of the furniture and the fabrication of the prototypes was a tricky business for Perriand. "Le Corbusier waited impatiently for me to bring the furniture to life," she reminisced in her autobiography, the only firsthand report of the creation of these pieces.

> I worked on the full-scale drawings with Pierre Jeanneret at the studio during the day and with Le Corbusier in the evening. . . . Time was passing. The chair designs we had worked and reworked could offer no evidence of their comfort during use since they didn't exist.
>
> Pierre cooked up some ephemeral armchairs, such as an inflated inner tube of a tire held in place by bars for reinforced concrete. . . . Another studio hand amused himself by sitting in the wire trash can which, crushed by his generous imprint, was transformed into both an armchair and a basket. . . .
>
> Corbu had enough of our pointless jokes. "Do what you must" is a Swiss Jura proverb. I took action. I gathered up the drawings and left the studio for as long as it took my craftsmen to fabricate the prototypes, although they were already very busy with my own creations [Perriand's furniture for the 1928 Salon installation]. Labadie [an iron worker in the Faubourg Saint-Antoine] made the metal frames in his workshop from odds and ends, then together we refined them into the first prototypes.

120 Studies for furniture, dated 1927. From *Oeuvre complète* (1929). **121** "Positions for Sitting." From *Précisions* (1930). **122** Sketches of living and dining room of the Villa Baizeau, Carthage, Tunisia, 1928. Gelatin print. Fondation Le Corbusier, Paris (8.503). **123** Sketch of interior of the Villa Ocampo, Buenos Aires, 1928. Ink. Fondation Le Corbusier, Paris (24.235). **124** Sketch of living room of the Maison Caneel, Brussels, dated 1929. Ink and pencil. Fondation Le Corbusier, Paris (8.529).

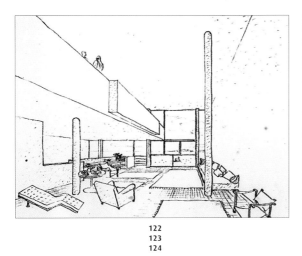

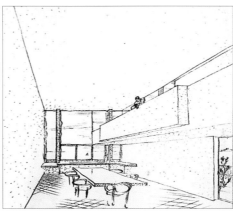

122
123
124

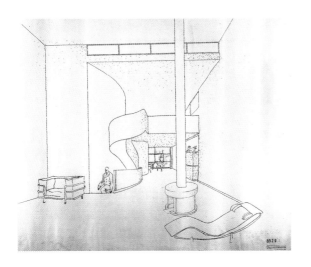

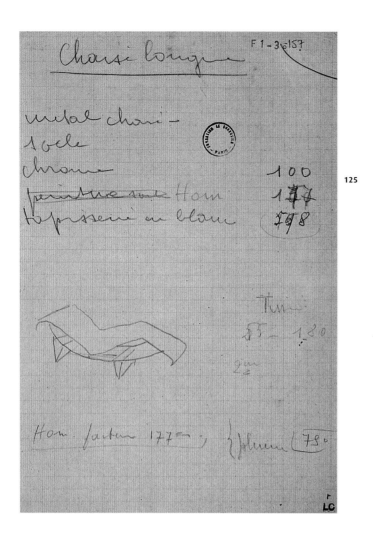

125

They were sent out for finishing—either chrome plating or lacquering.

I also bought metal springs from the BHV [Bazar de l'Hôtel de Ville, a Paris department store], and picked out at some furriers superb pony skins and skins of unborn calves, and for the chaise longue some canvas, which I asked a saddler to trim with a strip of pigskin, Hermès-style. . . . Everything was assembled in my studio at Saint-Sulpice: the chaise longue, sculpturally beautiful on its base, the chair with pivoting back for visitors, amd the large and small *confort* armchairs in natural leather. Four designs to which I added the revolving armchair made for my dining room, which was different in its conception. . . . Proud of the results, I invited Le Corbusier and Pierre Jeanneret to my studio, without letting on that the chairs were there, very much alive, ready to be sat on, faithful to our designs, as a surprise. They were overwhelmed. After several murmurs Corbu said at last, "They're stunning."[11]

At the same time as the furniture was being made and then photographed at the houses in Auteuil and Ville d'Avray, Perriand was fabricating pieces for other clients. Records show, for example, that a chaise longue was made for a client named Templier (probably the jeweler Raymond Templier), and around February 1929 an estimate for the chair with pivoting back, the dining chair, and the chaise longue was sent to the Marquise de Villavieja.[12] Notations in the archives of the Fondation Le Corbusier, unfortunately undated,[13] with Perriand's diagrams of the chaise longue (fig. 125), club chair in small (*fauteuil confort*; fig. 126) and large (*fauteuil canapé*) versions, chair with pivoting back (*siège dossier pivotant*), her own round dining chair and stool, and a simple U-shaped tubular-metal stool designated for the bathroom (fig. 127; which seems to be the same as one that appeared in Perriand's Salon d'Automne installation in 1928), list the costs for their manufacture, including the metal structural elements and their various finishes and the animal skins or woven materials and their fabrication. They also indicate that frames of the chair with pivoting back and the club chairs could be had in chrome or painted finishes, but the tubular steel of the other pieces was offered only in chrome.

The chaise longue is the most distinctive of the metal forms that the firm created (fig. 128). "Here is the machine for resting," Le Corbusier wrote in his lecture "The Undertaking of Furniture," which he published in 1930 in *Précisions*. "We built it with bicycle tubes and covered it with a magnificent pony skin; it is light enough to be pushed by foot, can be manipulated by a child; I thought of the western cowboy smoking his pipe, his feet up above his head, leaning against a fireplace: complete restfulness. Our chaise longue takes all positions, my weight alone is enough to

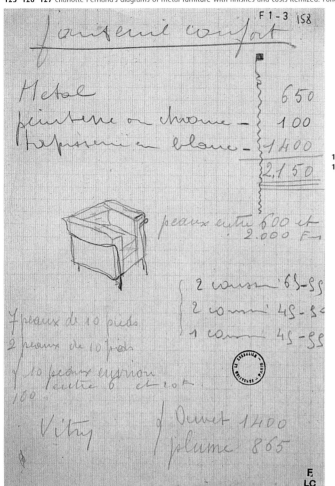

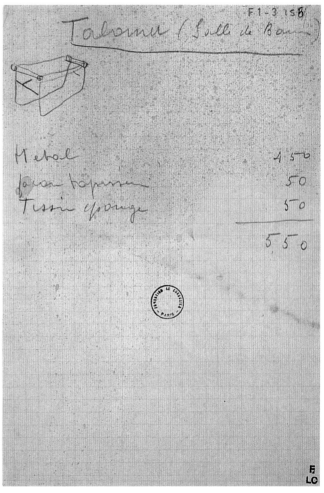

128

Mme Scholefield née Perriand,
MM. Jeanneret (C.-E.) dit le Corbusier et Jeanneret (A.-P.)

Pl. unique

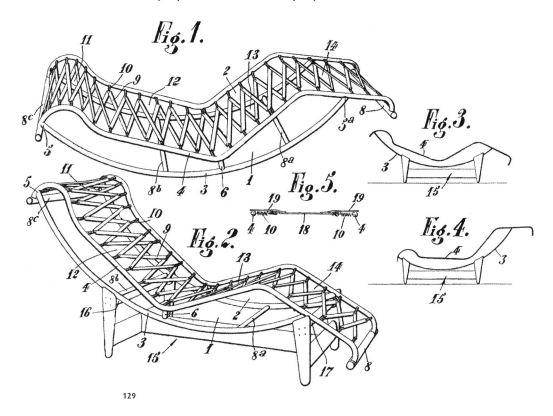

Fig.1.

Fig.3.

Fig.5.

Fig.2.

Fig.4.

129

keep it in the chosen position; no mechanism. It is the true machine for resting."[14] Relaxation in fact was one of the benefits of the chaise longue touted in the patent application submitted by Charlotte Perriand (under her married name, Scholefield), Le Corbusier, and Pierre Jeanneret, on April 8, 1929.[15] It was a multipurpose design, as the application demonstrates; the chaise is "capable of being used equally as an armchair or ordinary chaise longue, as a seat for relaxation, as a medical seat for resting the legs, and finally as a 'rocking-chair.'" These functions are demonstrated in the patent drawings (fig. 129): the frame is shown separate from the support for use as a rocking chair (Fig. 1), and poised on the support in three different positions, upright as an ordinary armchair or chaise longue (Fig. 2), horizontal for complete relaxation (Fig. 3), and inverted, the "medical" position, for the salutory elevation of the legs (Fig. 4). "One knows," the application explains, "that to obtain complete rest for the legs, it is necessary that they be at a level more elevated than the rest of the body."

The bowed, oddly shaped metal frame is crafted for maximum body comfort and described as presenting "a slightly bulging part for the head, and three flat surfaces disposed angularly and respectively destined to receive the back, the thighs, and the legs." The characteristic, somewhat orthopedic-looking structure had been worked out in a series of sketches that have been associated with the Villa Ocampo designs, dating to summer 1928 (figs. 130–32). The frames in these drawings are shown on a variety of bases, and in various positions. The final form of the base, designed, according to the patent, "in a general fashion in the form of a double T and notably including two rubber rollers on which the lower pieces of the sides of the seat can rest,"

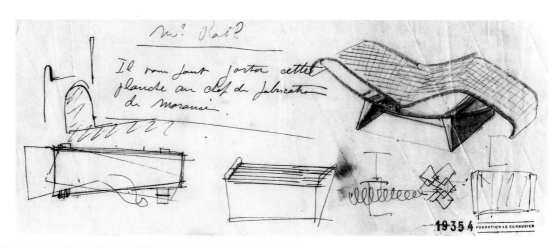

130
131

130 Studies for the chaise longue, 1928. Ink and pastel. Fondation Le Corbusier, Paris (19.354). 131 Studies for the chaise longue, 1928. Pencil and white chalk. Fondation Le Corbusier, Paris (19.355). 132 Studies for the chaise longue, 1928. Pencil and white chalk. Fondation Le Corbusier, Paris (19.357).

132

133 Sketch of living room of the villa designed for Paul Poiret, dated 1918. Ink. Fondation Le Corbusier, Paris (14.711). **134** "All Types of Furniture for the Sick & Wounded." Detail of an advertisement for Dupont, Paris. From *L'Illustration* (1925). **135** "Surrepos." Advertisement from *L'Illustration* (1926).

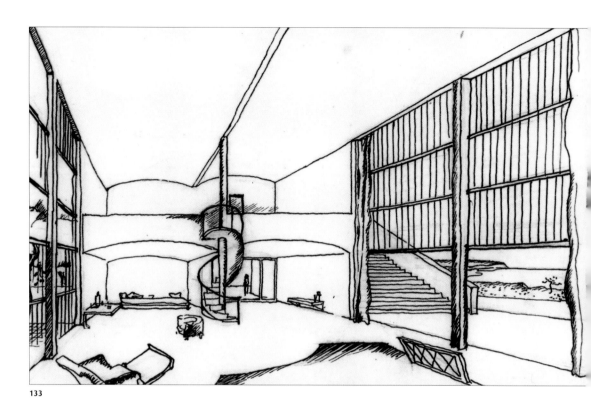

133

had not yet been determined when these preliminary drawings were done, and many possibilities are explored: a curved platform, two rectangular frames curving lightly as the sides meet the floor, two solid V-shaped supports, as well as the final design of four splayed legs connected with metal bars. Perriand recalls that the base gave the designers "a lot of anguish. After endless experiments and sketches, it was resolved along with that of our glass slab table designed for the Villa Church, which gave unity to our creations. The miracle was an ovoid section in lacquered sheet metal, found by chance in an aviation catalog."[16]

Conceptually, the chaise longue looks back to nineteenth-century rocking chairs and lounge chairs, such as Thonet's famous bentwood examples[17] and the ubiquitous Morris chair, with its back adjustable to several positions (which Le Corbusier discussed in *L'Esprit Nouveau* in 1923; he had depicted one as early as 1918 in his drawing for the villa of the couturier Paul Poiret; fig. 133). Invalid chairs that could be adjusted into zigzag configurations had been used since the previous century, and one, made by Dupont, a specialist furniture manufacturer in Paris, was advertised frequently in *L'Illustration* during the 1920s (fig. 134), shown with an attached apparatus for holding a book. But most influential was the Surrepos (Super-relaxing) chair of Dr. Pascaud, a widely advertised patented lounge chair with a head roll similar to the one used with the firm's chaise longue. Le Corbusier had known this chair at least since the middle of the decade when he had visited Dr. Pascaud and

considered including a special version for use in the Esprit Nouveau pavilion.[18] One Surrepos advertisement (fig. 135) describes and illustrates the advantages of the zigzag and adjustable design over that of a conventional, straight lounge chair. True relaxation was the point. "In the SURREPOS all parts of the body find support for their forms and their normal proportions: essential conditions for functioning well. Refreshing rest after your work or sport, serene meditation in the ambience you love: This is what the SURREPOS can give you." This advertisement features a photograph of a woman relaxing, which might have been the inspiration for the photograph of Charlotte Perriand in their lounge chair (see fig. 116); it also has an attached reading stand, an appendage that Le Corbusier had also considered in his 1927 drawing of seating types. The Surrepos chair could be adjusted to several positions, but required a complicated mechanism, while, as Le Corbusier pointed out, the chaise longue could easily be manipulated without any mechanism (although the user had to get up out of the chaise to do so).

The flexible criss-crossed blades that are shown in the patent drawings as support for the body "could be covered in any convenient upholstery," but an alternative form of upholstery was also offered (shown in Fig. 5 in the patent drawing) in which fabric could be attached with springs directly to the sides of the frame and banded with another piece of fabric. The form of the metal frame in the patent drawings, in which the sides join the head and foot bars at

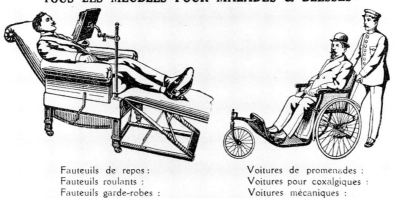

TOUS LES MEUBLES POUR MALADES & BLESSÉS

Fauteuils de repos :
Fauteuils roulants :
Fauteuils garde-robes :
Fauteuils articulés, etc.

Voitures de promenades :
Voitures pour coxalgiques :
Voitures mécaniques :
Voitures-fauteuils, etc.

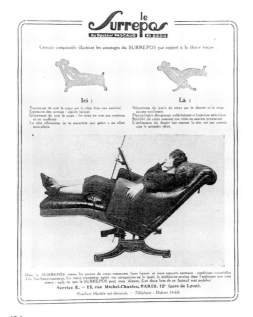

134
135

right angles somewhat in from their ends, matches that of an example without upholstery illustrated in the *Oeuvre complète*.[19] A chaise of this form appears in the photographs of the Villa Church, while another, upholstered in leopard skin with criss-cross blades below, was acquired by the Maharajah of Indore in Paris and later used in his bedroom in the modernist house built for him in India by the German architect Eckart Muthesius in 1930.[20] But in the chaise longue reproduced with Perriand reclining on it and the one shown at the Salon of 1929, the tubes at the top and bottom have been altered; they are no longer straight horizontal bars but form a continuous curve with the sides of the frame, the way the chaise longue has been constructed ever since.

With so much information at hand about the design and conception of the chaise longue, it is surprising that so little is known about the origin of the other two chairs in the group. There seem to be no drawings with the kind of ruminations that Le Corbusier had revealed in his sketches for the chaise longue, and since neither of the other two was patented, there is no official description of their construction or function. The club chair (fig. 136), in which five loose cushions are snugly contained within the boxlike frame—the "cushion basket" as they called it[21]—replaced the comfortable seating form previously filled by Le Corbusier with the upholstered Maple-type chairs. It was made in two widths, described by Perriand in her notes as *fauteuil confort* and *fauteuil canapé*.[22] As original in its conception as

136

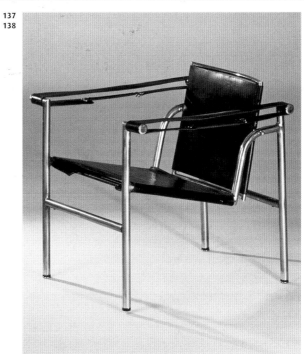

137
138

136 Club chair, 1928. Enameled metal and leather. Nationalmuseum, Stockholm. Raoul La Roche reluctantly acquired this chair. **137** Armchair with pivoting back, 1928. Nationalmuseum, Stockholm. This chair was also acquired by Raoul La Roche. **138** Armchair with pivoting back, 1928. Chrome-plated steel and leather. Vitra Design Museum, Weil am Rhein, Germany.

139

the chaise longue, it reverses the conventional structure of a chair, bringing the internal skeleton out, and making it the mainstay of the design. The frame of the club chair, in particular, was often lacquered, using a wide range of colors; La Roche's example, now in the Nationalmuseum in Stockholm (fig. 136), was brown with brown leather cushions, while the version shown at the Salon in 1929 had light green frames and dark gray cushions.[23]

While the club chair has no direct formal prototype, the armchair with pivoting back (figs. 137, 138) depends heavily on its model, a vernacular type that is found in many variants. In her autobiography, Perriand identified a chair with a jointed back that was used in the reading room in the Swiss Pavilion at the University of Paris as one that "may well have inspired" this design, a "chair with pigskin stretched on a removable frame of turned wood—the kind used for ages by *gauchos* in Latin America, who roll it up on their horses' saddles."[24] Others find the standard colonial or officer's chair used by the British since the nineteenth century as its direct source. A version called the Indian Chair, with a considerably higher back, was sold by Maple & Co. and appeared in its catalog during the 1920s (fig. 139). The typology of the chair with pivoting back, unlike the other forms, had only recently been added to Le Corbusier's vocabulary; its connection was demonstrated in the schematic furniture drawing in the perspective of the Villa Baizeau (see fig. 122), where Le Corbusier, if he had indeed found inspiration in the Indian Chair, had already reduced its tall pivoting back to the scale of the South American chair, repeated in the firm's version. But instead of completely rationalizing the rectilinear structure when it was prepared for metal fabrication, as we would expect from Le Corbusier's rhetoric and this drawing, the design was deliberately complicated into the fantastic creation that Peter Blake described as among "the wittiest, sexiest chairs designed in modern times."[25] The quarter-circle curve of tubular steel that interrupts the simple boxlike profile of back and seat, and was added "for no particular reason at all," as Blake reminds us, creates a tense, almost heart-stopping, moment in which the seat hovers in midair, an

implied cantilever that suggests a defiance of gravity. With this audacity, Le Corbusier, Jeanneret, and Perriand boldly demonstrated the strength of the new metal technology, their response to the pyrotechnics of cantilever seating that were then astonishing the world.

Two models of this chair are illustrated in the second volume of the *Oeuvre complète*, their method of upholstery seemingly the only distinguishing feature.[26] One has padded cushions attached to the frame, like the chair shown in the publicity shot of the Villa La Roche (and which La Roche later acquired), covered in blue silk and held with buttons (see fig. 137); two other padded chairs, which seem not to have buttons, are included among the furnishings of the Villa Church (see figs. 111, 112). The second model has the now familiar upholstery of hide or fabric wrapped around the frame and held taught by springs (see fig. 138). The arms of both versions are straps slipped over the tubes that extend at right angles from the structural frame of the chair.

Le Corbusier had planned for the first public showing of the metal furniture at the Salon des Artistes Décorateurs in May 1929, which would have closely followed the publication of Perriand's article in *The Studio*. It was then, however, that a number of progressive designers in the society, René Herbst, Robert Mallet-Stevens, Raymond Templier, and Perriand, among them, protested that their designs, which had been shown as a group in the previous exhibition and had attracted many favorable reviews, were not to be given a similar independent space again. They walked out and banded together to form a new association, the Union des Artistes Modernes, established in May 1929 (though the members did not exhibit together until 1930). Because of this, the debut of the firm's metal furniture was postponed, and May found Le Corbusier writing to the secretary of the Salon d'Automne to reserve space for the fall exhibition.

Lacking adequate funding for the presentation, the firm had come to an agreement with the Maison Thonet, the Paris affiliate of the Viennese bentwood furniture manufacturer, to underwrite the expenses of the Salon in return for the rights to distribute their metal furniture. Thonet,

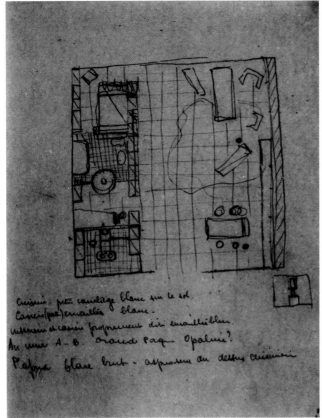

Cuisine: petite carrelage blanc sur le sol,
Cance (int.) émaillés blanc.
intérieur de casier proprement dit émaillable.
Au mur A-B. grand sac. Opalin?
Pafma blanc brut - aspirateur au dessus cuisinier

which had branched out and introduced an international line of metal furnishings, including pieces by Mies van der Rohe and Marcel Breuer, would now add the French models to its catalog. This arrangement is described on an order to the Forges de Strasbourg written some time early in summer 1929 (for delivery October 27) for the manufacture of the cabinetwork:

> FURNITURE
> 2 beds, of which one raised if possible.
> THE SEATS AND TABLES will be furnished by us.
> The FLOOR, and WINDOWS, will be furnished, possibly, by the ETABLISSEMENT SAINT GOBAIN.
> All other expenses of the stand are to be covered by the Maison THONET, which will be considered the presenter.[27]

Making all the furniture and getting ready for the Salon had cost the firm a lot of money, which it did not have, as Le Corbusier admitted to La Roche in a letter of October 1929: "This evening when I left you, I forgot to ask if you would keep the two chairs that are in your gallery [probably left there after the publicity photograph was taken]. We are preparing an important stand for the Salon d'Automne and we are in need of money. In the event that you would keep these chairs, I have decided with Madame Perriand (our associate for furniture) for you to pay the cost price. Included you will find the statement from Madame Perriand for each of the chairs. I would be grateful if you could give us a response before your departure, for the Salon opens on November 2."[28] This was a small part of the funds expended on this project over more than two years, but any income would have helped the finances of the firm. However, the sale was not quickly settled. Only a year later did La Roche begrudgingly agree to take the club chair: "After having examined the famous *Confort armchair A*," he wrote in a letter dated November 1930, "I want to establish that it is a bit shabby and consequently perhaps difficult to sell, especially at the price you have indicated to me, at Frs. 4230. I will keep it, although without enthusiasm."[29]

When Le Corbusier wrote that the firm was preparing an "important entry" for the Salon, he was referring not only to the new metal furniture but also to a new proposal for the arrangement of space in an apartment, a combination of large open areas that were of multiple, unspecified uses and small concentrated spaces that served clearly defined purposes, as is shown in a sketch for the presentation (fig. 140). The large, open-plan rectangle on the right is a loose multipurpose living space; the narrow, tightly packed area on the left includes two bedrooms, kitchen, and bath, with a freestanding cylindrical shower in the middle. The space was divided longitudinally by a long, high row of cabinets that separated the multipurpose living area, with its ceiling at full height, from the other rooms, which had dropped glass ceilings, with entrances simply breaks in the row; several half-height cabinets were used below the window on the other side, and others were in the kitchen and bedrooms. The large number of cabinets made of metal ordered from the Forges de Strasbourg provided for the variety of objects that would need storage space in a typical apartment. They were extremely flexible, consisting of cubic skeletons of aluminum, to which were attached exterior surfaces, doors, and shelves of metal or glass, some of which were painted.

The Salon entry presented an architecture in which privacy had been forgotten, in which the bedrooms were separated by an open bathroom, with a curved aluminum shower with sliding door in the middle and the frame of the bed extended over the headboard into a towel bar (figs. 141, 142). "This notion of freedom," Perriand wrote, "was intended to bring about different behavior patterns."[30] The arrangement was open to the same criticisms that had been levied at the free arrangement of the Stuttgart houses in 1927. "Are we, in the future," a Swiss critic had written, "to disregard the smell and the noise for the sake of an interesting spatial creation. . . ? Are these interpenetrating spaces a kind of program for living itself? Or is it all—as we

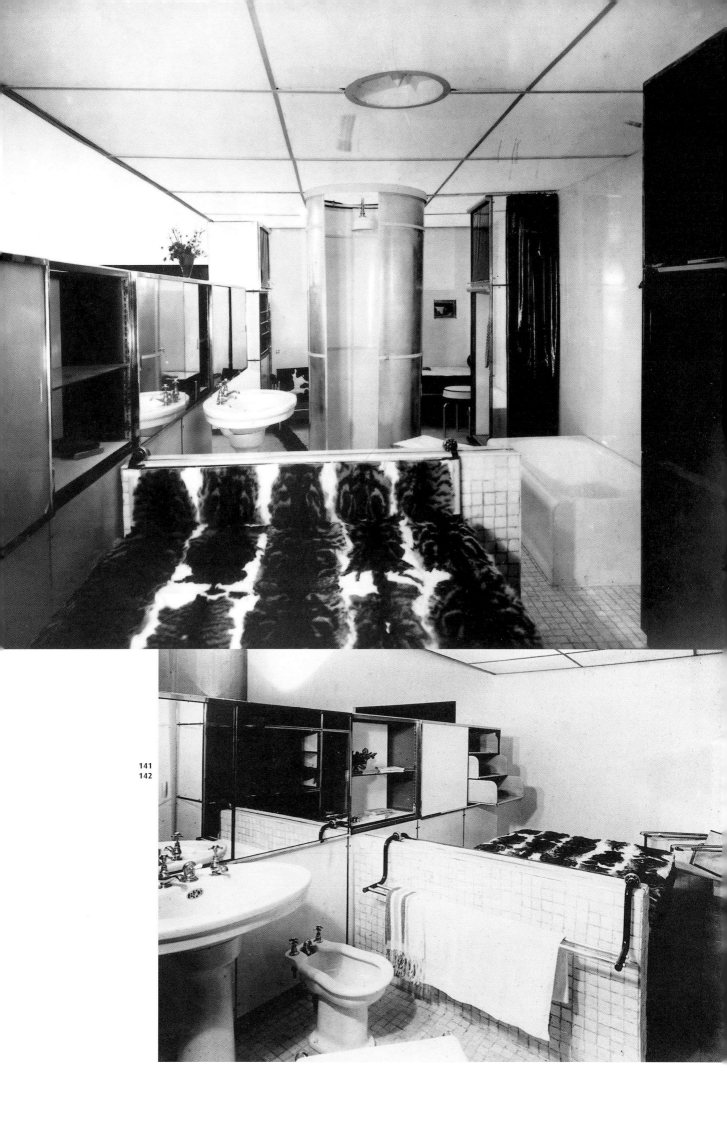

141
142

144

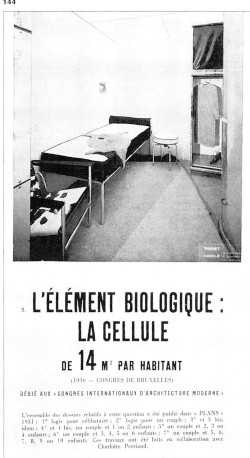

suspect—a mere paraphrase and continuation of studio life, where an improvised dinner stands on a wobbly table next to the easel, where if necessary the clatter of dishes and the strumming of the piano can be reconciled with desk work, and where bed is always there for a model and girl friend, complemented by bath and bidet? Or are we taking the whole thing too seriously, too pedantically?"[31]

The accessories were also deliberately planned to make a point. "The kitchen cabinets were decorated with saucepans, plates, and wooden racks with apples on them," Perriand added. "We placed a large cabbage on a stainless-steel counter in the middle of the room, like a bouquet of flowers [fig. 143]. . . . Pierre Jeanneret had brought along several issues of *L'Esprit Nouveau* to decorate the shelves, as well as his collection of delicate clay pipes. Beneath the strip window were other cabinets on which were displayed a dummy with moveable joints, pebbles, and glass Deyrolle test tubes with roses just in bloom. With this selection we were turning up our noses at the Decorative Arts."[32] Le Corbusier had nothing to do with such details of the Salon presentation because he was in South America at the time and, in fact, never saw the installation.

Although the overall size of the Salon display, 100 square meters, was way beyond that of a standard Salon entry, and far exceeded the minimal dwelling space of 14 square meters

145

per person that Le Corbusier was establishing in his work on machine-age urbanism (published as *The Radiant City*),[33] the small, defined spaces of the installation did fit these restrictions, and a photograph of the smaller bedroom area was used on the cover of the issue of his magazine *Plans* devoted to the minimal dwelling (fig. 144).[34] These investigations into considerations of tight space led to the research that would allow the firm to build vertical dwellings economically, and they tried many different schemes, including duplexes in the Clarté apartments built in Geneva and narrow floor-through units with exposures on opposite facades in the project for the rental apartments on the Rue Fabert in Paris (1932), which ultimately were resolved in the *unités d'habitation*.

While the broader spatial organization of the "Interior Equipment of a Dwelling" continued to be critical in the architectural thinking of Le Corbusier, the furniture shown at the Salon of 1929 had limited application in the firm's subsequent work, but took on a separate life of its own in the catalogs and presentations of Thonet and the other manufacturers later involved with it. The "equipment" appears sporadically during the 1930s in sketches of interiors for projects in development, sometimes almost half-heartedly, overwhelmed by the interior spaces (fig. 145). In practice, however, manufacturing costs were too high for the metal seating to be used in large commissions, despite efforts to reduce the costs. These pieces had not been conceived for mass production, relying too much on welding and other hand operations. The metal tables, however, were easier to manufacture and had a considerably wider use.

The metal furniture was only one of several options open to the firm. For example, in the reading room of the Swiss Pavilion at the University of Paris, which was designed and built between 1930 and 1933, the metal chair with pivoting back shares the space with the vernacular wood and leather version that may have inspired it, as well as with cane-top stools, the familiar Thonet-style bentwood office chairs, the firm's simple metal tables, and a large, heavily veined marble-top table (fig. 146). The furnishings of the

148

dormitory rooms, all identical, also combined wood and metal, with a freestanding cabinet and chairs of wood and a table and bed of metal (fig. 147). This strategy of relying on what was economical and readily available was applied to later commissions with similar programs, such as the cells at the monastery of Sainte-Marie-de-la-Tourette, where vernacular wooden chairs and tables, and simple shelving and cabinets served the needs of the monks (fig. 148).

But the firm continued their research by adapting previous type forms, designing a metal *canapé* (sofa) in 1934 for Le Corbusier's apartment (fig. 149) and creating a sequence of tables with wood and marble tops and metal pedestal supports that were used in their houses throughout the decade. In 1935, for the Exposition Internationale in Brussels, Perriand joined René Herbst and Louis Sognot in creating an exhibit, "Apartment of a Young Man," which included a study, a bedroom-bath, and an exercise room. Perriand alone was responsible for the study; she combined wood and metal furniture in her design, complementing her revolving armchair with her own inexpensive version of the chair with pivoting back made of straw and wood. She also worked out three other pieces using the firm's concepts: a slate table, blackboard wall, and a complex and particularized modular cabinet set on two pedestal legs, a return to the detailed conception of Innovation compartments. It included a range of drawers and filing sections of various

dimensions, and storage for a radio-phonograph and records (fig. 150). For Le Corbusier, the importance of this piece was the extreme refinement of the modular steel cabinet; it was a demonstration of the variety of forms that could be achieved and "an aesthetic affirmation of quality . . . capable of providing modern furniture with an elegance, with a 'line' of grand tradition." It called on French tradition not only for its elegance but also for its use of decoration: its doors and sides were elaborated with images extracted from *The Radiant City*. Le Corbusier attempted to "innovate with a technique of extreme precision and infinite resources (the zinc plate of photogravures) and the possibility of plastic and sentimental eloquence: the most beautiful damascening, and the possible use of poetic themes."[35] His endeavors in decorating (even if they were pedagogical, as in this exhibition piece) and his stated association with a grand tradition—the great French craftsmen of past centuries and their fine craftsmanship—reveal new ambiguities in his attitudes toward the decorative arts. Introducing pictorial elements and investigating the "possible use of poetic themes" was a complete about-face for an architect who only a decade earlier had declared that "modern decorative art is not decorated."

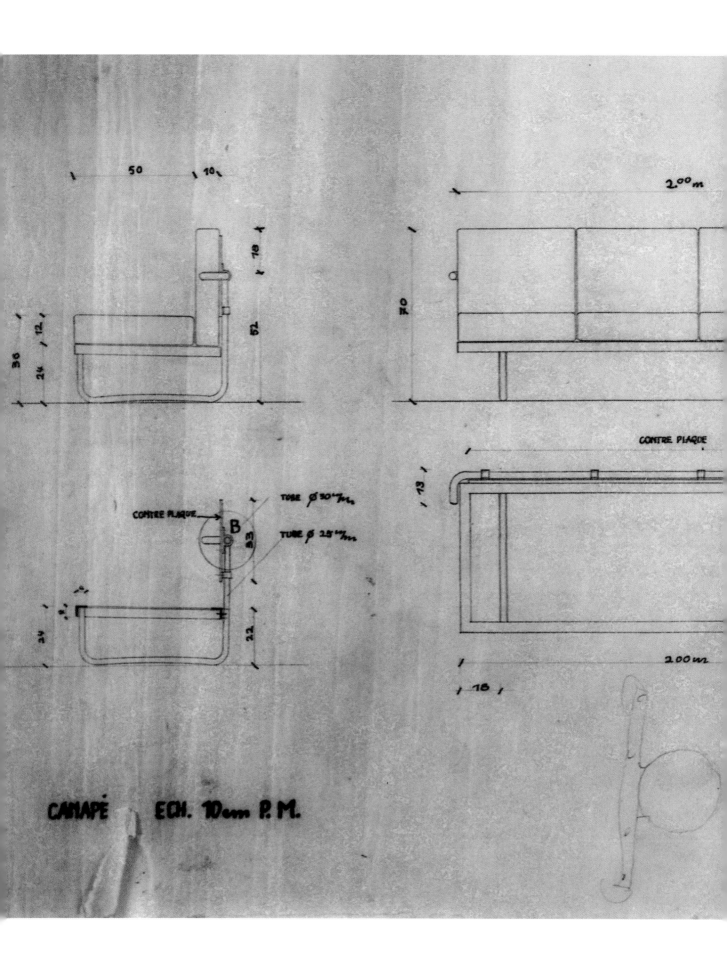

50 10

70 18

52

30 24 12

CONTRE PLAQUE → B 33

TUBE ⌀ 30 m/m

TUBE ⌀ 25 m/m

24 22

2.00 m

70

CONTRE PLAQUE

73

2.00 m

18

CANAPÉ ECH. 10cm P.M.

149 Drawings for a *canapé* (sofa) for Le Corbusier's apartment, dated 1934. Ink and pencil. Fondation Le Corbusier, Paris (19.358).

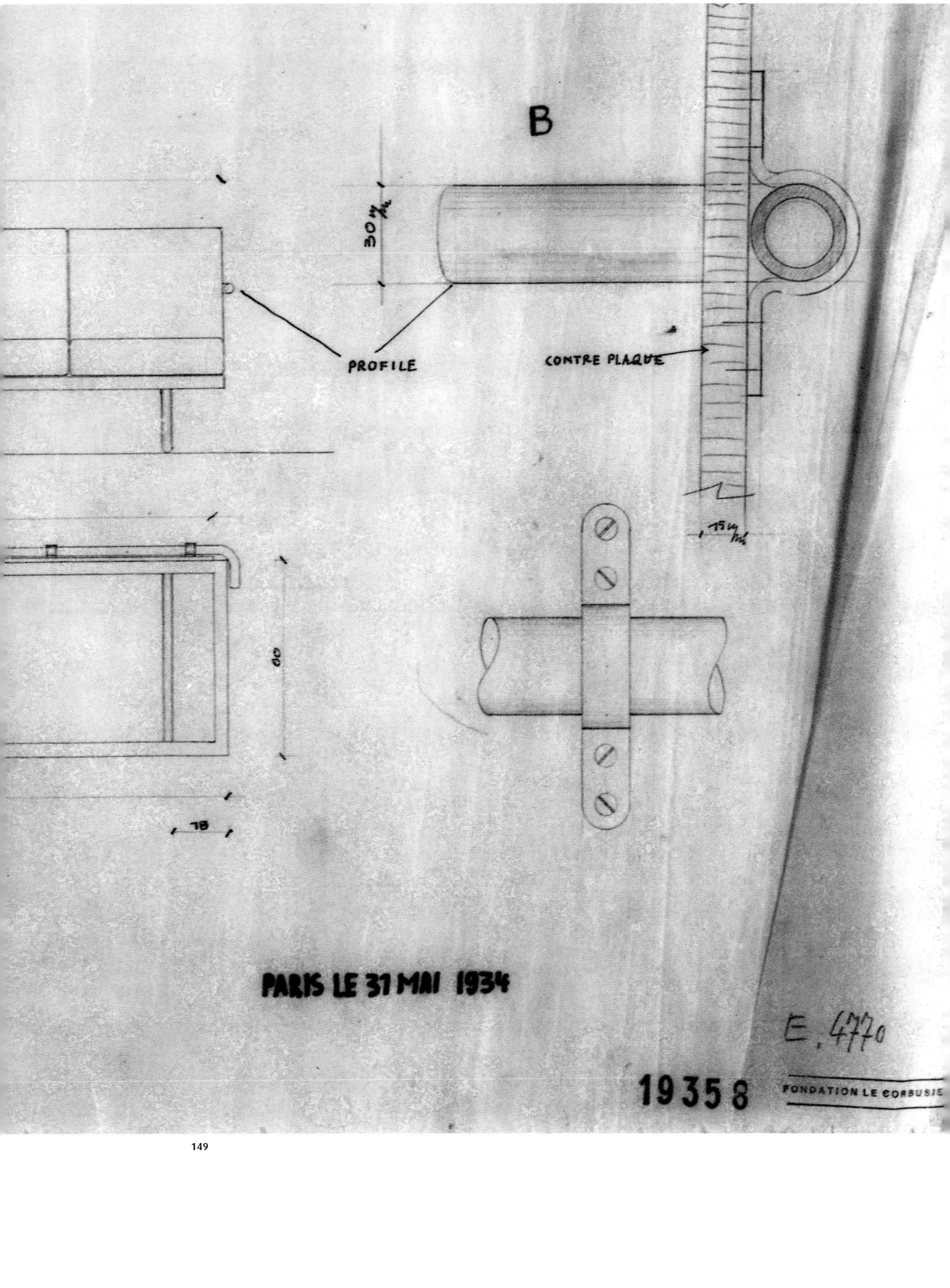

B
30 m/m
PROFILE
CONTRE PLAQUE
15 m/m
80
18
PARIS LE 31 MAI 1934
E. 4770
19358
FONDATION LE CORBUSIE

149

NOTES

1. Le Corbusier to M. Bonifay, May 18, 1928, FLC F1-3-55. "The space for which we have made our study," Le Corbusier wrote," is not what one would call a choice location, but it suits us perfectly because of its size and its circulation."

2. Le Corbusier, *The Decorative Art of Today*, trans. James I. Dunnett (Cambridge, Mass.: MIT Press, 1987), 92.

3. Le Corbusier, "A New Classification of Town Building, A New Dwelling Unity," in *Le Corbusier et Pierre Jeanneret: Oeuvre complète de 1929–1934*, ed. Willy Boesiger (Zurich: Editions H. Girsberger, 1935), 121.

4. John Gloag, "Wood or Metal?," *The Studio*, January 1929, 49–50.

5. Charlotte Perriand, "Wood or Metal?," *The Studio*, March 1929, 279.

6. See Akio Izutsu, *The Bauhaus: A Japanese Perspective and a Profile of Hans and Florence Schust Knoll* (Tokyo: Kajima Institute Publishing Co., 1992), 44–47.

7. Le Corbusier to Alfred Roth, July 21, 1927, reprinted in Alfred Roth, *Begegnung mit Pionieren* (Basel and Stuttgart: Birkhäuser Verlag, 1973), 34.

8. See, for example, Guy de Brummel, "Salle à manger moderne 1928," *Maisons pour Tous*, September 15, 1928, 147; Marcel Valotaire, "The Paris Salons," *The Studio*, September 1928, 201, 203.

9. H.-A. Martinie, "Le XVIIIe Salon des Artistes Décorateurs," *Art et Décoration*, June 1928, 165, 166.

10. Le Corbusier to Lucio Costa, January 27, 1964, FLC D1-3-162.

11. Charlotte Perriand, *Un Vie de crèation* (Paris: Editions Odile Jacob, 1998), 32–33.

12. Templier's chaise longue is listed in the undated final accounting for the metal furniture and the Salon d'Automne installation, FLC T2-6-202; copy of undated estimate to the Marquise de Villavieja, FLC F1-3-38-39.

13. FLC F1-3-156-162.

14. Le Corbusier, *Precisions on the Present State of Architecture and City Planning . . .*, trans. Edith Schreiber Aujame (1930; reprint, Cambridge, Mass., and London: MIT Press, 1991), 118.

15. French patent no. 672.824, applied for April 8, 1929, received September 24, 1929, published January 7, 1930, with a duration of fifteen years.

16. Perriand, op. cit., 32.

17. Some Thonet rockers also had book holders attached; see *Thonet Bentwood and Other Furniture: The 1904 Illustrated Catalogue* (1904; reprint, New York: Dover Publications, 1980), 54.

18. Dr. Pascaud to Le Corbusier, April 16, 1925, FLC A2-13-225.

19. *Le Corbusier et Pierre Jeanneret: Oeuvre complète de 1910–1929*, ed. W. Boesiger and O. Stonorov, 4th ed. (Zurich: Les Editions d'Architecture Erlenbach, 1946), 157.

20. See Reto Niggl, *Eckart Muthesius 1930: The Maharajah's Palace in Indore, Architecture and Interior* (Stuttgart: Arnoldsche, 1996). The furnishings, including this chaise (lot 215), were sold by Sotheby Parke Bernet, Monaco, May 25, 1980.

21. Perriand, op. cit., 22.

22. FLC F1-3-158, 159.

23. Arthur Rüegg, "Anmerkungen zum *Equipement de l'habitation* und zur *Polychromie intérieure* bei Le Corbusier," in *Le Corbusier: La ricerca paziente* (Lugano, 1980), 161, n. 18.

24. Perriand, op. cit., 53.

25. Peter Blake, *The Master Builders* (New York: Alfred A. Knopf, 1960), 67.

26. *Oeuvre complète de 1929–1934*, 44.

27. FLC F1-3-64-67.

28. Le Corbusier to Raoul La Roche, October 21, 1929, FLC P5-1-286.

29. FLC P5-1-287; the costs of fabrication and purchase price are verified in the undated, final accounting for the metal furniture and the Salon d'Automne installation and related documents in FLC.

30. Perriand, op. cit., 37.

31. *Das Werk* 19 (1927): 263; translated in Karin Kirsch, *The Weissenhofsiedlung: Experimental Housing Built for the Deutscher Werkbund, Stuttgart, 1927* (New York: Rizzoli, 1989), 118.

32. Perriand, op. cit., 37.

33. *La Ville Radieuse*, published in 1935; see Le Corbusier, *The Radiant City: Elements of a Doctrine of Urbanism To Be Used as the Basis of Our Machine-Age Civilization* (New York: Orion Press, 1967).

34. "'La Ville Radieuse' et l'élément biologique: La cellule de 14m² par habitant," *Plans* 9 (1931): 49–64.

35. *Le Corbusier et P. Jeanneret: Oeuvre complète de 1934–1938*, ed. Max Bill (Zurich: Editions Dr. H. Girsberger, 1939), 122.

150 Modular cabinet shown in Charlotte Perriand's study in the "Apartment of a Young Man" installation at the Brussels international exhibition, 1935. From *Oeuvre complète* (1939).

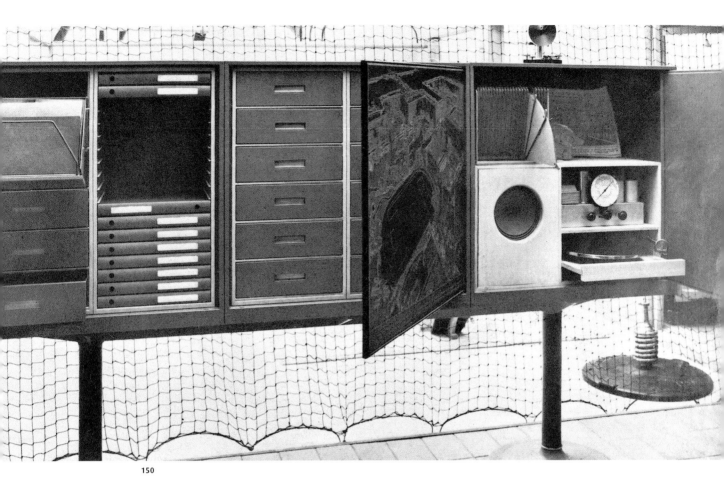

150

6

Thonet, Weber,
and Cassina Models

production furniture

Using pieces that had been shown at the Salon d'Automne in 1929 and other stock manufactured under the supervision of Charlotte Perriand, which the company acquired as part of their agreement to cover expenses for the "Interior Equipment of a Dwelling" presentation,[1] Thonet Frères began to market the group's tubular-metal furniture in 1930, and as soon as was possible printed a brochure devoted exclusively to it.[2] The pieces they sold, numbered B301 to B308 in the brochure, included the chair with pivoting back (B301); three models of Perriand's revolving stool, with back and arms (B302), with back but no arms (B303), and with neither (B304); bathroom stool with removable seat made of Turkish toweling (B305); chaise longue (B306; a 1933 Thonet Frères brochure shows a version, B306-O, with the chaise mounted on an oval rocking base[3]); simple glass-top table (B307); and glass-top table with ovoid base (B308). The club chairs, which were never given "B" numbers, do not appear in the brochure and do not seem to have ever been manufactured by Thonet or its affiliates, the reason perhaps that so few early examples are known. A document in the Fondation Le Corbusier archives that includes diagrams of these pieces along with the Thonet model numbers and a breakdown of the cost of each piece according to the upholstery that could be chosen for it—canvas, special fabrics, and artificial, high quality, or deluxe leather (fig. 151)—must have been used by Perriand in conjunction with clients referred by the firm to Thonet.[4]

The firm's tubular-metal designs also appeared almost immediately in catalogs issued abroad by Thonet-Mundus, the multinational company to which Thonet Frères belonged. After having purchased its first metal designs in 1928, Thonet-Mundus had moved quickly to dominate the market in modern metal furniture as it did in bentwood furniture; the following year it had acquired Standard-Möbel,

the German company that had been set up to produce and market Marcel Breuer's models, and the addition of his chairs, tables, beds, desks, and other utilitarian tubular-metal forms made Thonet the leading international manufacturer and supplier of metal designs even before they added the French lines.

In 1930–31 Thonet-Mundus, from its headquarters in Vienna, issued a portfolio-catalog of steel furniture in German and English[5] that illustrated both the designs that had been previously acquired in Germany and a group of new works manufactured in France, not only those of Le Corbusier, Jeanneret, and Perriand, which had already been published in the French brochure (and carried the same model numbers), but also a sizable number by the architect-designers Béwé (Bruno Weill, director of Thonet Frères), A. Guyot, and André Lurçat. The pieces from the firm that were included were the armchair with pivoting back, revolving armchair (ascribed here to Le Corbusier, Jeanneret, and Perriand), revolving stool, bathroom stool (misidentified as being by Béwé; fig. 152), chaise longue (fig. 153), and the two glass-top tables. The portfolio cover (fig. 154) was designed to demonstrate that modern steel furniture was both international and universal by showing the work of French and German designers combined in the same settings: the Le Corbusier, Jeanneret, Perriand armchair with pivoting back is grouped with a Breuer armchair around one of his glass-top tables in a living room arrangement, while Perriand's revolving armchair is shown before a Breuer typewriter table, and Breuer's cantilever chair is set before an unattributed desk (possibly by Guyot) in an office vignette. Now that one firm was distributing metal furniture from both countries, this may have been an attempt to redress the enduring rivalry between France and Germany in the field of design. A recent development had been the

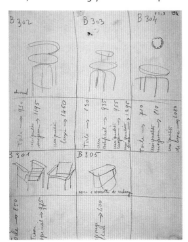
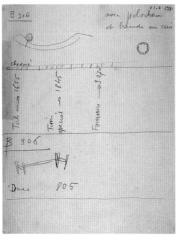

151

151 Charlotte Perriand's worksheet showing metal furniture with Thonet model numbers, finishes, upholstery materials, and costs. Fondation Le Corbusier, Paris (1-3-194, 193). **152** Bathroom stool (model B305) from Thonet Stahlrohrmöbel catalog (1930–31). Bauhaus-Archiv, Berlin. **153** Chaise longue (model B306) from Thonet Stahlrohrmöbel catalog (1930–31). Bauhaus-Archiv, Berlin.

B 305
Thonet

B 306
Thonet

Arch. Le Corbusier / P. Jeanneret / Ch. Perria

152 153

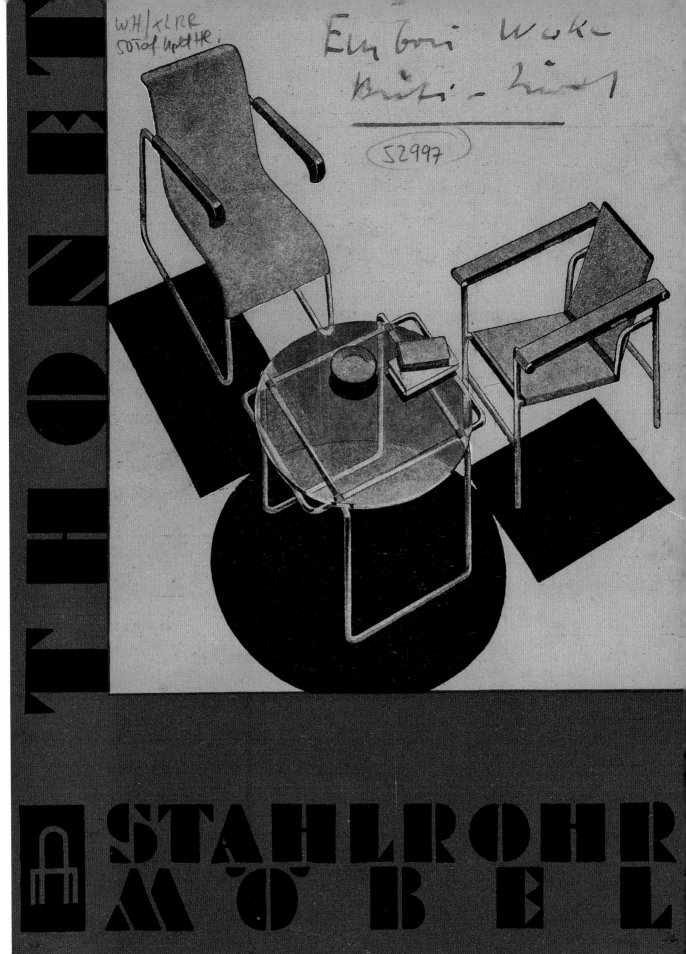

154

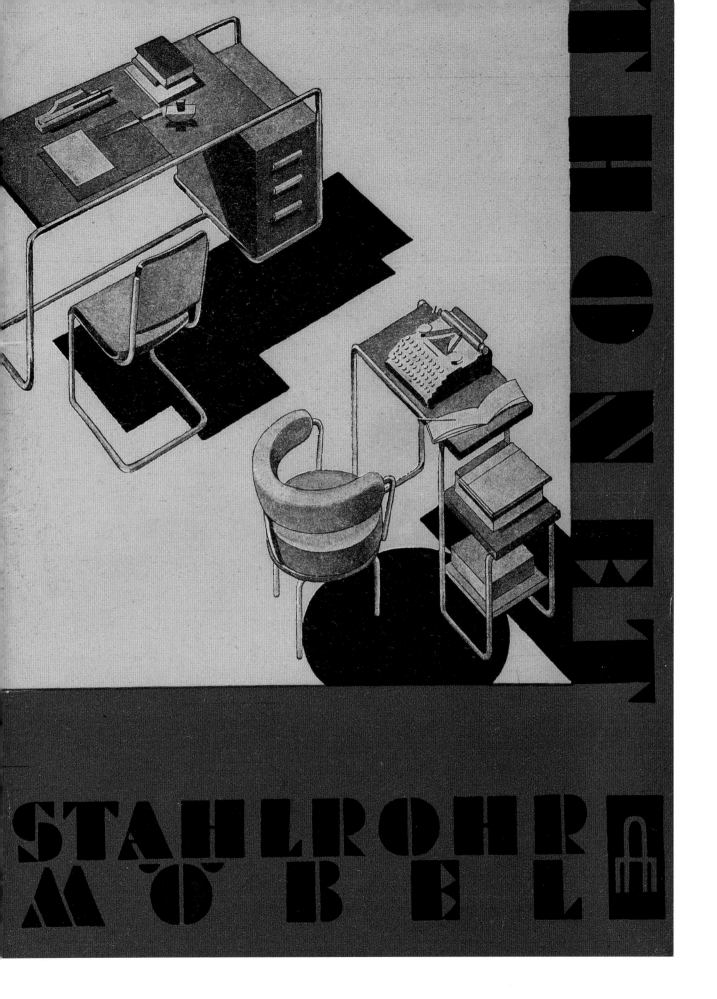

THONET

STAHLROHR
MÖBEL

exhibition of the work of the Deutscher Werkbund in Paris at the Salon of the Société des Artistes Décorateurs in 1930, a signal from the older French group (whose progressive members had left the previous year to form the U.A.M.) that their society was now ready to enter the modern era with a display of metal designs, even if they were of foreign origin.

The Thonet-Mundus catalog offered all its tubular-steel models in the same materials. The finishes they made available were both shiny chrome plate and lacquer in a range of colors that would have horrified postwar adherents to the notion of functionalism whose view of this production depended on the legacy of black and white illustrations and the austerity promulgated by the exponents of Machine Art and the International Style in the 1930s. The virtues of both finishes were carefully described in the catalog:

> CHROME-PLATED. The precision steel tubes out of which our tubular steel furniture is made are first copper-plated, then nickel and eventually chrome. Considering today's technical standards chrome-plating guarantees optimum protection against rust and should thus be preferred to a simple nickel-plating. Chrome-plated tubular steel furniture has a platinum-like, subtle blueish-white colour and a shiny surface. . . .
>
> LACQUERED. In this version the tubular steel is treated in

a specific chemical process. The lacquer offers excellent rust prevention. Furthermore, it renders the furniture resistant to bumping and scratching. This type of tubular steel furniture can be delivered in the following colours: lacquer red, brick red, lemon, cream, green, blue, violet, chocolate, silver grey, white, black, and pea green as well as in a silver and gold bronze."[6]

Thonet's chrome and lacquer fit in well with the finishes that had already been used by Le Corbusier, Jeanneret, and Perriand, although many of the colors offered were considerably removed from the Purist palette preferred by Le Corbusier. The upholstery was equally bold as the lacquer: gray, rust, brown, orange, red, green, blue, black (fig. 155), and yellow are listed as the colors available for the stretched fabric that was used, a durable weave called *Eisengarn* (iron cloth). "This material is especially woven for our purposes," the catalog explains, "and does not stretch so that it is perfectly suited for the seat and backrest. Many experiments have proven that no other fabric can compare with the results of the one we use."[7] In the case of the chaise longue (fig. 156), an *Eisengarn* cover stretched around the frame greatly simplified the earlier design of the upholstery, eliminating the need for the criss-cross blades described in the patent. Although a considerable number of examples with leather or hide upholstery are known, they were not among

the standard options offered by this international Thonet catalog, pointing to the disparity of frame and upholstery found in Thonet and Thonet-licensed models depending on when and where they were made, and the difficulty of attributing these pieces to specific manufacturers.

The disposition of the rights to market these designs internationally cannot have been very clearly stated when Thonet was negotiating with Le Corbusier's firm for the furniture. This was the basis of a controversy that was to last three decades. Even after Thonet Frères had taken over sales, in May 1930 Le Corbusier was discussing international distribution with a representative of the Berlin firm Deutsche Stahlmöbel, and a draft contract was sent to him that would have given the German company exclusive rights to fabricate and sell the chaise longue throughout the world except in France.[8] At the same time Le Corbusier was also writing to Thonet Frères with concerns about international distribution, a matter that had to be referred to Vienna.[9] Thonet had historically been able to produce large quantities of furniture by licensing production on a country by country basis, but it meant that the details of construction and quality of manufacture, as well as materials and finishes, were not always consistently maintained. Le Corbusier never understood how these licenses worked, and by 1934 he had become totally frustrated over the seemingly uncontrolled, even if relatively modest, nature of the manufacture of their furniture in Switzerland and Czechoslovakia, and probably in other countries as well. Le Corbusier took the opportunity of a cordial invitation from the Thonet licensee in Czechoslovakia, Mücke-Melder Werke, to explain his position: "I am very gravely disappointed by the issue concerning the exploitation of the models of our furniture. I came to an agreement with M. THONET for the sale of my models in France and abroad. All the results that have been reported to me periodically by the THONET office are terrible. So terrible that I must admit that my models have not been successful. Is it true or isn't it? I am not sure. You told me you were a licensee of THONET. Would you perhaps be so kind as to let me know if our models are delivered to you or sold by you in a regular & lucrative fashion."[10] He could not have been very happy with the answer, for he learned point blank that the works were not doing well, and was told that the public preferred the simpler, more direct designs of Mart Stam, the Dutchman credited with creating the first modern metal cantilever chair in 1927.[11] By the mid-1930s, however, the firm's works rarely appeared in Thonet's catalogs or advertisements, and sales seemed to have dwindled accordingly. Thonet never seems to have been very attentive to these pieces, and if the statement attached to

a postwar note to Le Corbusier is accurate, sales dropped very rapidly after the initial burst of interest in metal furniture.[12] Yet, even though the sales were not impressive, there had been repeated problems with piracy from the time their designs were first introduced. As early as July 1930 Thonet Frères had written to inform them that a chair "in all points similar to your model of the revolving armchair" and a "chaise longue depending on the same principles as yours"[13] appeared in the catalog of the current decorative arts exhibition in Stockholm.

By the beginning of the war, manufacture of metal furniture had essentially ceased, as metal was a restricted material necessary for the war effort. Thonet-Mundus had been split up; the descendants of Thonet retained rights to produce Thonet designs in Europe east of the Rhine, while the international Thonet firm, which in 1940 as war approached was able to establish itself in the United States, held the rest of Europe and America as its territory. Directly after the war, design interest had changed, with organic styling based on Scandinavian products or the new methods developed in America for molding plywood supplanting the earlier interest in metal. In 1949 Le Corbusier, still smarting under the terms of the 1930s agreement with Thonet, returned to the matter of production when he wrote to Jeanneret, "I intend to try to put back on track the two armchairs and the chaise longue from 1929 that Ch. Perriand and the two of us collaborated on. I would like you to tell me precisely the contractual state of affairs with Thonet in a way that I can do what is necessary in this regard, and if the occasion arises, you can send me the working drawings of the project. It is well understood that I will send this in our common interest without being sure, however, that it will come to better solution than what you have done. But who knows?"[14] Nothing concrete came of this attempt, but his continued frustration turned into outrage in 1952 when "a rich Brazilian" told him that he had seen a chaise longue in a store that sold modern furniture in Zurich: "There, they are making this chaise longue and I know nothing about it! And I have never seen a penny from the royalties. I find that unbelievable!" he wrote to the architect Willy Boesiger in Zurich, one of the editors of the *Oeuvre complète*, describing his plight and enlisting his aid. "I would like to have a chaise longue for my wife, who needs to rest with her legs elevated," he continued somewhat pathetically, suggesting that Le Corbusier had never even owned a model of the chaise longue himself and underscoring his continued faith in the "medical" benefits of the design. "Could I ask you to make inquiries and protest strenuously on my behalf demanding that they pay the royalties and send me a chaise longue here as indemnity."[15] It was Wohnbedarf, the department store in Zurich long known for its progressive interior design, that had caused the problem; they offered to send him a chaise longue, which they said was of greater value than what royalties on the few pieces they sold would have come to, and gave him a realistic assessment of the slight interest there was then in this type of work. They included a résumé of how the control of the firm's designs had deteriorated and become fragmented:

> Before the war, your model was found in the Thonet catalog. For Switzerland, Thonet had given the manufacturing license to the Swiss corporation Fabricants de Meubles en Fer, a corporation composed of
> Embru S.A., Rueti/Zch
> Bigla S.A., Biglen/Be
> Fabrique Bâloise de Meubles en Fer S.A., Sissach (Bâle)
> An illustration of your chaise longue was found in the catalogs of these firms. We ourselves bought it from these firms. We do not know if on their part Thonet paid you license fees with regard to the undertaking in question. After the war, this furniture was not being made anywhere—thus we took it upon ourselves to have the few isolated pieces that we have need for made by our house metalworker, without being aware of the need for a license.[16]

Le Corbusier must have been resigned to the situation, for in 1954 he could write to Wohnbedarf again, asking to buy another chaise longue like the one they had sent. Then as a postscript he added "an observation of a technical nature": "The base is of such a nature that it impedes raising the lower part of the chaise longue to its best advantage, which is unfortunate, for the benefit of this chaise longue is precisely to allow one to have one's feet very high. From my point of view, the back part of the base should be 54 centimeters instead of 52 cm, which would permit more extensive gliding in the direction of the base of the chaise. If you can realize this modification for the new order I would be delighted."[17]

The problem of the firm's commitment to Thonet continued to bother Le Corbusier. Finally in 1959 he resolved the issue to his own satisfaction, summarizing his position in a memo to the firm's business manager, A. P. Ducret, and telling him that Heidi Weber, an interior designer and gallery owner in Zurich, and the publisher Hans Girsberger were to issue the chaise longue, and that Charlotte Perriand had already sent drawings to Willy Boesiger so that he could oversee fabrication of the furniture.[18] "My opinion," he wrote, "is that Thonet had no right as assignee to unknowns

without my authorization. From 1929 to 59, that is to say after thirty years, I have the right to take back the manufacture of my chaise longue."[19]

Late in 1959, Weber, who had recently become completely taken with the art of Le Corbusier, gave him an exhibition of paintings, and presented the tubular-metal furniture along with it. Although the memo mentions only the chaise longue, Weber issued a small edition of four of the furniture designs (with new model numbers)—large club chair (LC101), small club chair (LC102), chair with pivoting back (LC103), and chaise longue (LC104)—all under the name Le Corbusier with no mention of either Perriand or Jeanneret, as is seen in the sales booklet of loose sheets titled *Le Corbusier 1929: Sièges, Sitzmöbel, Chairs*.[20] The booklet describes the tubular frames as being made of nickel- or chrome-plated steel, and the frames of the club chairs were also offered in black; the iron support of the chaise was available in black or in black with the longitudinal crosspiece in white. The chaise and the armchair with pivoting back could be upholstered in pony skin or fabric, while the loose horsehair and down cushions of the club chairs were covered in leather or fabric and supported underneath by a spiral spring mesh.

The following March, Ducret wrote to inform Perriand that "at the initiative of Le Corbusier, the Société POLYTECH [in Paris] has entered into an exclusive contract with Madame Heidi WEBER . . . for the manufacture and the sale of the steel furniture previously manufactured and sold by THONET under your name and under that of Le Corbusier (with the exception, however, of the revolving armchair). Le Corbusier has thus asked me to let you know that your earlier agreements are still in effect and that from the profit derived from the sale of the furniture, one third will be paid to you, the second third going to Pierre Jeanneret, and the third to Le Corbusier."[21]

Although Ducret carefully noted that the furniture had been sold by Thonet under the joint names, he did not mention that Weber was marketing it only as the work of Le Corbusier, as shown in the sales booklet, and advertising it that way as well.[22] This could not have been to Perriand's liking, but later, in an interview, Perriand was resigned to the situation as it was, recognizing that "the name 'Le Corbusier' sings—three names don't have the same resonance."[23]

In 1965 the four pieces were brought into larger production by the Italian manufacturer Cassina in collaboration with Le Corbusier, the designs based apparently on "those that Le Corbusier redrew for mass production before his death."[24] The four pieces, for which the system of model numbers introduced by Weber was simplified (from LC101

156 157

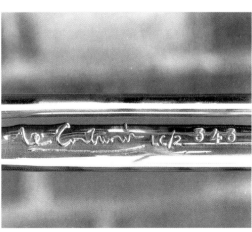

159

to LC1, LC102 to LC2, etc.), were made in nickel-plated or enameled tubular steel with leather or pony skin upholstery, and were signed and numbered (fig. 157). Additional models were added in 1974, 1978, 1985, and 1998. In 1978 the entire collection was revised in collaboration with Perriand and the Fondation Le Corbusier, and more colorful versions were added "using colours in accordance with shades foreseen in the original palette of Le Corbusier"[25] (fig. 158). Each piece in what is called the "Cassina Masters" series was to bear a signature in the form of a trademark, the "Masters" logotype (incorporating Le Corbusier's emblem), production number, and an identity card, while Perriand agreed that it was enough to have the labels read: "Création 1929, Le Corbusier-Jeanneret-Perriand."[26] In addition to the metal seating, expanded to include sofas and Perriand's own designs, and the two tables from the 1920s (fig. 159), Cassina models now include a pedestal table and a version of the casiers (fig. 160), which are related to designs from the 1930s.

The production of this furniture is still expanding. Not only are additional pieces being added to the authorized production by Cassina, but reproductions and imitations by many different manufacturers seem to appear every day. This has brought down the price of all models, including the authorized versions, making these items even more widely accessible. But the question of design attribution still remains, and in most cases, regardless of who manufactured it, this furniture still "sings" with the name of Le Corbusier alone, even if subsidiary information included with the pieces may credit the contribution of the other two codesigners.

NOTES

1. Undated Thonet Salon accounting, titled "Stock à Vendre," FLC F-1-3-190.
2. Christopher Wilk, *Thonet: 150 Years of Furniture* (Woodbury, N.Y., and London: Barron's, 1980), fig. 136.
3. Ibid., fig. 135.
4. FLC F1-3-193-194.
5. *Thonet Stahlrohrmöbel: Steckkartenkatalog (Thonet Tubular Steel Furniture: Card Catalog)*, (1930–31; facsimile reprint, Weil am Rhein, Germany: Vitra Design Museum, 1989).
6. Ibid.
7. Ibid.
8. See Deutsche Stahlmöbel to Le Corbusier, May 29, 1930, FLC T2-6-196.
9. As indicated in Thonet Frères to Le Corbusier, P. Jeanneret, & Ch. Perriand, Paris, July 7, 1930, FLC F 1-3-30. The exact nature of the concerns is not known.
10. Le Corbusier to Mücke-Melder Werke, May 9, 1935, FLC F1-3-174.
11. Mücke-Melder Werke, May 14, 1935, FLC F1-3-175; see Werner Möller and Otakar Máčel, *Ein Stuhl macht Geschichte* (Munich: Prestel, 1992).
12. FLC F1-3-188.
13. Thonet Frères to Le Corbusier, Charlotte Perriand, and Pierre Jeanneret, July 19, 1930, FLC T2-6-198.
14. Le Corbusier to Pierre Jeanneret, March 31, 1949, FLC F1-3-186.
15. Le Corbusier to Willy Boesiger, July 7, 1952, FLC F1-3-223.
16. Wohnbedarf to Le Corbusier, September 10, 1952, FLC F1-3-224.
17. October 27, 1954, FLC 1-3-197.
18. Copies of the drawings dated December 1958 with Boesiger's label affixed are in the Fondation Le Corbusier.
19. Le Corbusier to A. P. Ducret, January 8, 1959.
20. *Le Corbusier 1929: Sièges, Sitzmöbel, Chairs* (Zurich: Heidi Weber, 1959), catalog leaflet. Fondation Le Corbusier, Paris, pamphlet files.
21. A. P. Ducret to Charlotte Perriand, March 23, 1960.
22. In *Zodiac* 6 (1960).
23. Quoted in "Charlotte Perriand Looks Back (and Forward)," *Architectural Review*, November 1984, 66.
24. Franco Cassina, quoted in Rita Reif, "Young Men Hope to Sell Le Corbusier Furniture in Volume," *New York Times*, March 14, 1967, 50.
25. *"Cassina: I Maestri": Le Corbusier* (Milan: Cassina, 1988).
26. Quoted in "Perriand Looks Back," 66.

7

Creating the
Modern
Apartment House

the radiant city

The modern building ideas that Le Corbusier first formulated in the early 1920s in the *immeubles-villas* project—an amalgamation of private, self-contained, modular living spaces with garden terraces, adjoined horizontally and stacked vertically into urban housing blocks—culminated in the series of high-rise apartment communities (*unités d'habitation*) he designed after the war, most importantly and most successfully the first one he built in Marseilles, between 1946 and 1952 (fig. 161). Four other *unités* followed, three in France, at Rezé-les-Nantes (1953–54), Briey-en-Forêt (1957–61), and Firminy (1962–68), and one in Berlin (1956–58), all somewhat smaller in scale and for varying reasons less successful. In these buildings Le Corbusier extended his earlier model of private dwelling units stacked into high-density, high-rise, low-cost housing to include an array of communal functions—commercial establishments, leisure facilities, and basic civic services—that broadened its components and created an integral community, or vertical garden city, based on the model of a collective. The idea for this had emerged from Le Corbusier's visit to communal housing schemes in Moscow in 1928 and 1930, when he was engaged on the construction of the mammoth Centrosoyuz office complex there. Both the notion of introducing a variety of residential services and the concept of apartments arranged along interior corridors, or "streets in the air," which give a unique character to the *unités*, can be traced back to revolutionary housing in the U.S.S.R.[1] Le Corbusier's concept was to create a sense of intensely private, family housing within a larger community, the idea going back to the experience of his first visit to the Carthusian monastery of Galluzzo, which made him "conscious of the harmony which results from the interplay of individual and collective life, when each reacts favourably upon the other. *Individual and collectivity* comprehended as fundamental dualism."[2] But its success derived from the fact that the project had what Le Corbusier called an "appropriate size,"[3] that is, it had a large enough critical mass for its communal functions to work efficiently and economically.

Le Corbusier chose the ocean liner, which housed, fed, and entertained thousands of passengers in a very restricted space, as the design paradigm for his new concept of communal housing. He undertook to adapt many of its features, from the organization of space to the organization of people's lives within it, to this project. Building on a tight scale made his high-rise vision economically feasible, and like the ocean liner he described in his book *The Radiant City* (1935), it worked within "astonishing physical limitations because its communal services are rigorously organized, because the living quarters are stripped of all parasitical

161 *Unité d'habitation*, Marseilles, 1946–52. Fondation Le Corbusier, Paris.

Telle est la coupe d'une maison

162
163

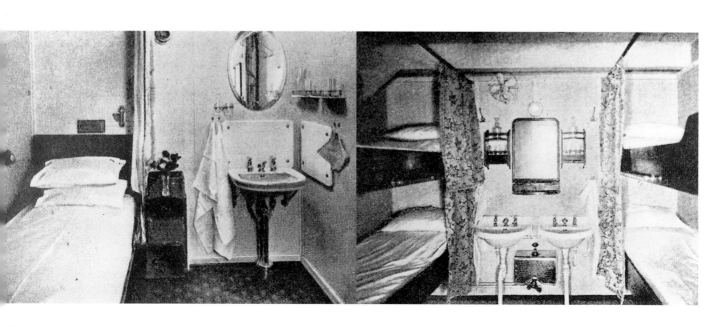

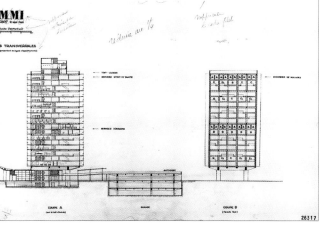

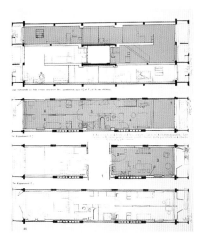

164 165

elements, and because life aboard . . . is governed by an intelligent use of innovations that *permit a solution of the space problem*, on the one hand, and that REJECT ALL WASTE, on the other."[4] The illustration captioned "Cross-section of a 'floating apartment house'" that appears in *The Radiant City* (fig. 162) shows the many decks of a ship with their private staterooms, public spaces (lounges, dining rooms, and open and covered promenades), and service areas that inspired the division of living and communal spaces employed in the apartment block in Marseilles: the interior streets that provide access to the apartments; the floors that make available commercial services such as shopping, laundry, and catering; and the roof deck, which offers a place for recreation and relaxation in its gymnasium, 300-meter track, outdoor stage, and children's play area.

The model of the ocean liner was to extend to individual apartments as well, and in *The Radiant City* Le Corbusier used photographs of cabins to "show the results of strictly observed economy"; he did not illustrate these as models for actual apartment units but as examples of the efficient organization of space and equipment (fig. 163). The core of his apartment design, which dictated, and provided for, what he thought were the basics for modern living, was "a human unit, a cell, that is biologically good in itself (in conformity with the individual's needs)."[5] Le Corbusier was able to design extremely tight but efficient cells for his high-density housing by adopting the minimal dwelling space of 14 square meters per occupant proposed at the 1930 Brussels International Congress of Modern Architecture (CIAM). In conjunction with Charlotte Perriand, he worked out series of calculations breaking down the space within apartments using the 14-square-meter standard, and created floor plans and sketches for modular apartments derived from these calculations, which were first published in 1931 in the journal *Plans*[6] (and partially reprinted in *The Radiant City*). The apartments they sketched out varied greatly in size, from a small efficiency for a bachelor to a large unit for a family with ten children. In his text, Le Corbusier posed the inevitable question: "Will it be possible to live comfortably on the proposed basis of 14 m² of floorspace

per occupant?"[7] He answered it by returning to the example of luxury liner staterooms—which took up considerably less space—as proof of its viability, without however noting in his argument that residency on a ship was only temporary. Living for a long time in such restricted spaces, narrow rectangular rooms with no nooks or crannies that might provide some sense of privacy, would demand both tight control of personal actions and relations and a strict limitation on the accumulation of possessions, the latter suiting Le Corbusier's Spartan temperament well.

The large, rough concrete building in Marseilles, a controversial postwar reconstruction project financed with public funds, is set firmly on splayed piers, or pilotis, on what was then uncultivated land in the outskirts of the city between the Mediterranean Sea and a ring of bleached, rocky hills. The scheme put into place there encompasses a seventeen-story slab with 337 apartments on fifteen residential floors housing some 1,600 inhabitants and conceived as one of a series of similar buildings in a park setting (the others were never built). The massive building is a complex arrangement of interlocking duplex apartments, each based on the concept of the "Citrohan" house and the Esprit Nouveau pavilion, and tried out in a somewhat different version in the Clarté apartments in Geneva in 1928–32. The Marseilles apartments are built over and under the interior streets, an efficient scheme that requires elevators to stop only at every third floor (figs. 164, 165). Removed from the abstract beauty and brutality of the honeycomb exterior of Le Corbusier's concrete construction, the interior streets have been domesticated into townscapes with deliberate, narrative elements that defy comparison to any of his other building concepts. With a wacky and wonderful notion meant to create a simulacrum of village streets lined with private houses, the long corridors are clad with prefabricated concrete panels inset with washed Mediterranean stones that suggest a row of rusticated masonry facades (fig. 166).[8] Each private entranceway in this theme interior has a letter slot, a large protruding box for deliveries, and a light above the door, all suggesting the routine of village rather than apartment life, where the postman

166 167

168 *Unité d'habitation.* Lamp in elevator landing. **169** Design for a lamp, dated 1952. Pencil. Fondation Le Corbusier, Paris (31.868).

168

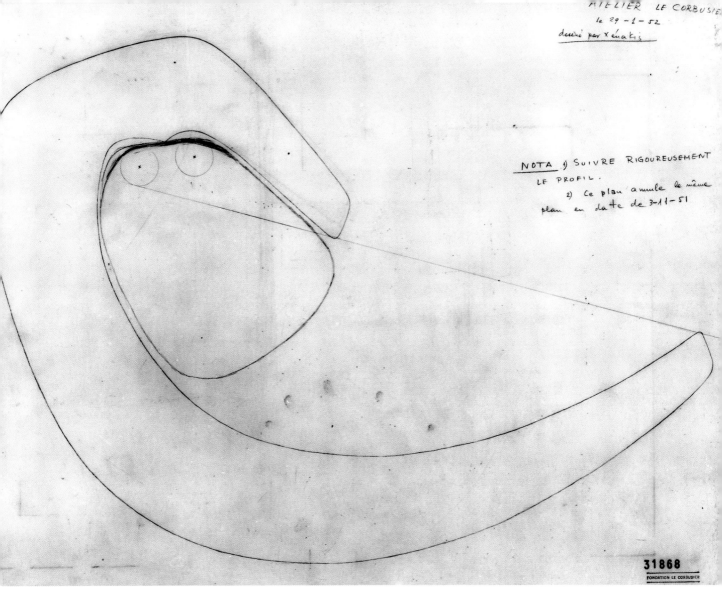

ATELIER LE CORBUSIER
le 29 - 1 - 52
dessiné par Xenakis

NOTA 1) SUIVRE RIGOUREUSEMENT
LE PROFIL.
2) Ce plan annule le même
plan en date de 3-11-51

31868
FONDATION LE CORBUSIER

169

brings the mail each day, shopkeepers make home deliveries, and lights welcome visitors to every house. The over-door lights are the only means of illumination for the streets, and the wide, low corridors are perpetually dim, set forever at a dusk that hastens residents to the warmth, and light, of their own dwellings. The only natural light that even attempts to seep into the corridors comes from the large windows in the central elevator landings, offset from the street, where the masonry panels of the interior and the brutalist poured concrete of the exterior interact. At night the landings are barely lit by oversize, baroque sheet-metal lamps in the shape of an apostrophe, each supported on a pole and held with two prongs (figs. 168, 169); fluorescent tubes within the circular core illuminate the pebbly metal surface below, which glows with a cool, even, but dim, light. Overlaying this village fantasy is a festive color scheme (in Le Corbusier's words, "an extraordinary and mysterious symphony of colors"[9]), designed to individualize each entranceway and each floor. The inset entranceway panels, which include the doors with long, natural wood handles and the service elements, are painted in slightly muted primaries and secondaries following the sequence of the color wheel—red, orange, yellow, green, and blue—but no violet. (The colors today, repainted over some fifty years, probably do not exactly replicate the originals.) The large delivery boxes that punctuate the view down the

street and compose the only colored element that is seen when the corridor is viewed centrally are painted identically on each floor, and are different from those on adjoining floors in order to distinguish one floor from the other.

Entrances from the interior streets to the duplex apartments are on the level of the kitchen and dining area, the heart of the household; in one, the preferred layout (fig. 170), the kitchen-dining area adjoins the two-story living area and the terrace, and one must climb the metal staircase to reach the parents' bedroom and children's rooms (narrow spaces divided by a movable blackboard partition that opens for play and closes for study and sleep; fig. 171); in the other layout, the entrance and kitchen-dining area are on a sort of balcony and one descends the staircase to the living room and parents' and children's bedrooms. Each apartment is a floor-through, with a two-story terrace on the living room side and a one-story terrace off the children's bedrooms on the other, affording breathtaking views of both the Mediterranean and the hills. Le Corbusier tried to modify the strong Mediterranean light coming into the apartment with horizontal sun breaks (brises-soleil) on the exterior of each balcony, and he used light as an experiential device, drawing one from the dimly lit interior street to the moderate light of the entrance and dining area to the brightness of the living room with its window wall (pan de verre) and terrace.

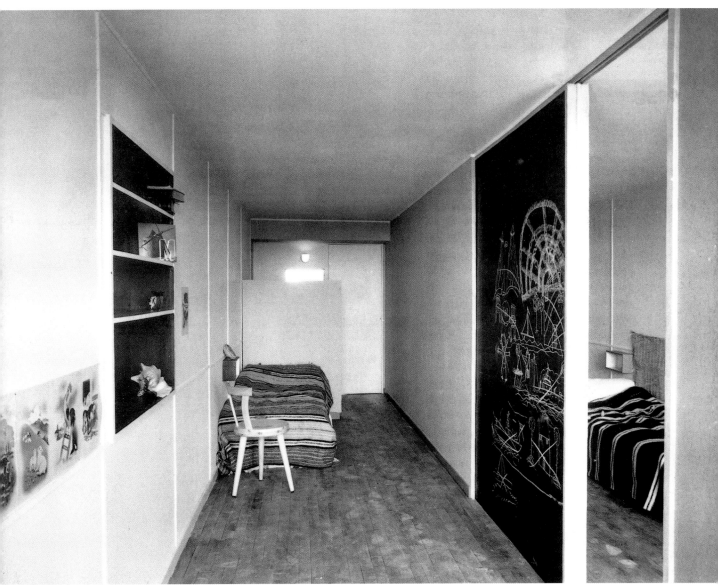

170 171

In his essay "Town Planning. The Theory of the 7 V [Seven Ways]," Le Corbusier articulated the symbolism of the apartment unit he created as "the shelter of the family group" to correlate the new open living plan designed for the modern vertical city with elemental aspects of the home and the traditional type spaces found in conventional housing (fig. 172).

> The "Fire," the "Hearth." One has come in from outside (1); one has come into somebody's house (2); one finds the ancient "fire," the "hearth" of tradition. The mistress of the house is preparing the meal by the stove, the family is around her, the father and the children. They are all around the "fire" where they spend those hours of the day consecrated to the institution of the family, the mealtimes (3). The "fire" can just as well be electric or gas. The kitchen is in, and a part of, the livingroom, but the livingroom is opened to the sun, the space, and the greenery by means of a loggia which is really a brise-soleil (4), a portico, such as Socrates advocated, which allows the inhabitants of the house to savour the good things which a Bountiful God dispenses to men. It gives coolness in summer and warmth in winter. . . .
>
> The family group has its own bath room with showers and W.C. together in one place and storage space, with summer and winter cupboards for clothes and linen in another. The ironing board (5 and 8). At (6) closed off by a door is the parents bedrooom, and at (7) closed off by two doors, two childrens bedrooms each with one or two beds. A movable partition allows the two rooms to be joined. They also have a brise-soleil opening to the sun, space and greenery. This makes up the plan for a "machine for living in."[10]

This was the didactic equivalent of the symbolic objects he had previously added to the photographs of his buildings. His childlike drawing seems to return everything to the basics, and although he clearly describes a cell unit that could be located hundreds of feet in the air, he shows it as if it were at ground level on its own private turf.

The immensity of the planning and construction of the Marseilles housing block meant that Le Corbusier had little time to work out details of the project himself. He created an overlapping organization, Atelier des Bâtisseurs (Builders Workshops), called ATBAT, to oversee the areas of administration, works management, engineering and technical research, and architectural work.[11] And he called Charlotte Perriand back after her return from Asia, where she had spent the war years, specifically to design the interiors, particularly the kitchen (which had been conceived under his

Le groupe familial
" le feu "
" le foyer "
l'appartement
le logis

172

direction earlier by his associate André Wogenscky). As delin-
eated at Marseilles, the kitchen was to become a focal point
in the life of the French family, signified by the innovative
divider with pass-through. Now that the kitchen was only
half separated from the dining area, the mother would
always be in touch with her family (fig. 173). The modern
kitchen incorporated cooking, cleaning, refrigeration (an ice
box, which was accessed directly from the interior street
and refilled with daily ice deliveries), storage, and air ven-
tilation and waste disposal elements engineered into the
building's waste-handling system. The oak-framed kitchen
units with sliding and hinged paneled doors painted in different colors (fig. 174) had aluminum work surfaces with
inset ceramic-tile countertops, and such additional specialized features as pullout cutting boards, soap holder, and
vegetable storage bins.

Originally the kitchen was to have been built as a complete prefabricated unit, and Perriand worked with the
proposed manufacturer, CEPAC, to iron out all the details:
"The firm CEPAC seemed the most able to meet our needs.
They carried out the work diligently down to the slightest
detail. All that remained was the estimates. . . . This first
prototype did not pass muster."[12] In order to cut costs, the
studio gave up the idea of a complete prefabricated unit
and instead pieced together all of the elements of the
kitchen from separate sources. However, CEPAC did try to
market their prototype, well before the completion of the
building in Marseilles. This was the subject of a clipped
memo of clarification to Perriand from Le Corbusier outlin-
ing the history of the kitchen concept, and warning her that
the studio would have to be involved if the kitchen were to
be marketed commercially.[13] He distinguished between the
scheme of Wogenscky (which he called "cuisine atelier Le
Corbusier, type 1") and the CEPAC model (which he called
"Cuisine-Atelier Le Corbusier, type 1—interpretation Charlotte
Perriand—fabrication").

The apartments are completely faced with plywood panels, with some painted in primary colors but most left with
their natural wood grain exposed. The narrow, two-story
living room faces onto a glass wall, which opens onto a terrace over a broad sill one step up. Fitted with cushions, the
sill adds seating area to a tight space and is useful whether
the doors are open or closed (fig. 175). The terraces have
ledges made of openwork and built-in concrete tables, and
the dividing walls between apartment terraces are painted
a sequence of bright colors. Except for the many cabinets
found in the kitchen, hallways, and bedrooms (many with
long natural handles like those used on the front doors),
the built-in bookshelves, and the threshold that serves for

seating, no furniture was designed for the apartments. The
model apartments were completed instead with furniture
that was already in production, designed by Charlotte Perriand and Jean Prouvé (who also made the prefabricated
wood and metal staircases), along with a lamp designed by
Le Corbusier (fig. 176).

The service floors have mixed uses: retail space to provide daily necessities, medical offices, a hotel for residents'
guests, and communal services, with the interior streets following the same color system as the other floors. A public,
"exterior" gathering place was fitted with large windows
and concrete benches inset with colored tile in the form of
small teardrops (like those used on the rooftop benches),
and a row of the baroque lamps (fig. 167). And inside and
out, Le Corbusier added depictions of his Modulor, the measuring system he created and depended upon to achieve
harmony in architecture, and which was the organizing
measure by which the entire building was conceived (fig.
177). The *unité* in Marseilles was the first project totally
built according to the Modulor. Le Corbusier described the
system as "a measuring tool based on the human body and
on mathematics. A man-with-arm-upraised provides, at the
determining points of his occupation of space—foot, solar
plexus, head, tips of fingers of the upraised arm—three
intervals which give rise to a series of golden sections."[14]
The building was constructed using just fifteen measurements derived from the Modulor series of mathematical
calculations that are shown next to the figure in the standard depiction. "This immense building, 140 metres long
and 70 metres high," Le Corbusier wrote in appraisal of the

175

Modulor system, "appears familiar and intimate. From top to bottom, both inside and out, it is to the human scale."[15] To emphasize its centrality to the building's creation, the Modulor figure was cut from stone and poured in concrete on its exterior, painted on glass on a panel in the entranceway (fig. 178), and cut out from plywood on one of the service floors.

For reasons both political and economic, the *unité* in Marseilles was the most successful of Le Corbusier's projects for mass housing, although it went through rough times when it was first built, the subject of lawsuits and the distrust of the local population, who condemned it as a "Loony Bin." But there has always been a core group of residents faithful to the social concept, and the *unité* continues to function, although many of its residents are no longer the government employees for whom the building was originally intended. At the celebration thirty years after its inception, Perriand visited many apartments and noted how some things had changed over the decades: "Dishwashers and refrigerators with freezers instead of the original ice compartments stocked everyday by suppliers from the interior street. All these new technologies," she wrote, "had indeed liberated women, but also required more space."[16] Some of the communal facilities became less important, with individual washing machines, for example, supplanting the need for laundry rooms. Perriand found that the nursery-school teacher Lillette, who, faithful to Corbusian ideals, had taught her youngsters "to draw pictures of wonderful flat-roofed radiant houses," had finally retired, and children were now copying a poster image of a traditional house with pitched roof and small shuttered windows. "Farewell radiant life," she lamented, "it is all over." But it isn't, although the level of services provided at Marseilles is inconsistent, and communal aspects of the building seem to have become less important. The demographics have changed, with more affluent professionals coming in, and the current generation's demand for larger spaces has been met by some residents who have bought two adjacent units and joined them together.[17] With its tight but well-conceived dwelling spaces, its amenities made to meet daily needs, and the colorful streets that symbolize a village community, Le Corbusier's planning still has its following. The Socialist *unité* retains its conceptual validity and could have renewed applications in developing countries willing to invest in socially progressive housing, even if the numerous feckless impersonations of the structure that were built throughout the world over the past half century have given it a bad name.

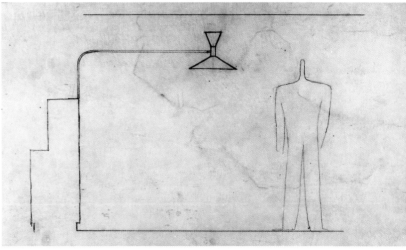

176

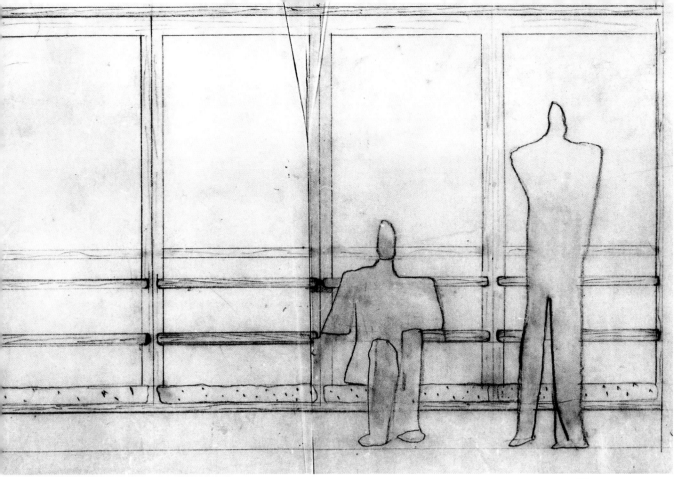

177
178

NOTES

1. See Jean-Louis Cohen, *Le Corbusier and the Mystique of the USSR: Theories and Projects for Moscow, 1928–1936*, trans. Kenneth Hylton (Princeton, N.J.: Princeton University Press, 1992), especially 124.
2. Le Corbusier, *The Marseilles Block*, trans. Geoffrey Sainsbury (London: Harvill Press, 1953), 45.
3. Ibid., 41.
4. Le Corbusier, *The Radiant City: Elements of a Doctrine of Urbanism To Be Used as the Basis of Our Machine-Age Civilization* (New York: Orion Press, 1967), 117.
5. Ibid., 143.
6. "'La Ville Radieuse' et l'élément biologique: La cellule de 14m² par habitant," *Plans* 9 (1931): 49–64.
7. *The Radiant City*, 117.
8. This type of facing was used again by Le Corbusier on his museum in Tokyo.
9. *Le Corbusier: Oeuvre Complète 1946–1952*, ed. W. Boesiger, 3rd ed. (Zurich: Editions Girsberger, 1961), 205.
10. Ibid., 95.
11. See André Wogenscky, "The Unité d'Habitation at Marseille," in *The Le Corbusier Archive*, vol. 16, ed. H. Allen Brooks (New York and London: Garland Publishing, and Paris: Fondation Le Corbusier, 1983), IX–XVII.
12. Charlotte Perriand, *Une Vie de crèation* (Paris: Editions Odile Jacob, 1998), 240.
13. See Ruggero Tropeano, "Unité d'habitation de Marseille, 1946–1952," in *Le Corbusier: Une encyclopédie* (Paris: Centre Georges Pompidou, 1987), 200–203.
14. Le Corbusier, "The Modulor: A Harmonious Measure to the Human Scale Universally Applicable to Architecture and Mechanics," in *Modulor I and II*, trans. Peter de Francia and Anna Bostock (Cambridge, Mass.: Harvard University Press, 1980), 55.
15. *Oeuvre Complète 1946–1952*, 179.
16. Perriand, op. cit., 242.
17. See Lesley Hussell, "Le Corbu," *Architectural Review*, June 1997, 76–82.

8

afterword

"One of the most important concerns of modern architecture," Le Corbusier wrote at the close of the 1930s, "is to determine precisely the function of materials. In fact, alongside the new architectural masses, which are determined by the means of new techniques and by a new aesthetic of form, a precise and original style can be conferred by the intrinsic property of the materials."[1] Almost as soon as the decade began, Le Corbusier had launched out in a new direction, jettisoning the cool, anonymous geometrics of Purist harmony and order for a new and original style that called on rough and irregular materials, sometimes serendipitously, and that was specific to locale. This new approach could be seen as early as 1930 in the Errazuris house in Chile, made of tree trunks and rough lumber, left exposed and unpainted; in the Villa Mandrot in La Pradet in the south of France (1930–31), with fieldstone walls; in his own apartment and studio in Auteuil, with its party wall of irregular brickwork and its vaulted ceilings; and in a diminutive weekend house at La Celle-Saint-Cloud in Paris (1935), the most complex of the group, with a composition of both natural and manmade materials (fig. 179), which he articulated in all its diversity in the elevations (fig. 180) and lovingly enumerated in his *Oeuvre complète*: fieldstone masonry, natural outside, white inside; walls of plate glass and glass brick; whitewashed plaster, or plywood paneling with natural grain; vaulted ceilings faced with plywood on the inside, covered with earth and sod above; white ceramic tiles on the floor; fireplace and chimneypiece of natural brick; and a dining table made of light cipolin marble.[2] Unlike the smooth, crisp interiors of the Villa Savoye, with its flat white and colored walls that dematerialized under the dazzling light, these buildings had a tactile richness and a weighty solidity, emerging from the use of heterogeneous materials that allowed place, tradition, and technique a role in the design. The pattern set in the 1930s continued into the postwar period with the Maisons Jaoul in Neuilly (1954–56; fig. 181) and with the Villa Sarabhai in Ahmedabad, India (1955), where, as Le Corbusier said, he set out "to reestablish contact with the noble and fundamental materials of architecture: the brick, friend of man; rough concrete, a friend also; white coatings, friends of man; the presence of intense colors provoking joy, etc.,"[3] aspects of vernacular building that he had found so fascinating on his voyages through Eastern Europe when he was young.

Inside and out, the surfaces of his houses took on individual meaning, resonating with associations, with the richness of their materials and the artisanal techniques of their construction. Fieldstone also was used as a focal element in buildings otherwise modernist in conception, such as the

179

180

Swiss Pavilion at the University of Paris, and a similar emphasis on the elaboration of surface appeared in his reinforced-
concrete structures in the natural imprints of the wooden
forms used for pouring concrete, which he manipulated for
deliberate effect to create simple repeating and opposing
patterns, stripes, and chevrons. Sigfried Giedion, in discussing
the "hopes and fears" of architecture in the 1960s in the enlarged edition of his influential *Space, Time and Architecture*,
spoke of Le Corbusier's "architectural revitalization of the
wall." He cited the *unité* in Marseilles as the "pathfinder,"
where "a plastic modeling of the wall was already accom-
plished. Its surfaces are interwoven with large-scale rhythms
of horizontality and verticality," for which Le Corbusier "did
not smooth away the marks and hazards of the form work
and the defects of hand craftsmanship." But Giedion also
saw this as a dangerous trend in modern architecture, ob-
serving "everywhere a tendency to degrade the wall with
new decorative elements."[4]

Surface elaboration of any sort had always been a problem for Le Corbusier. He was ever fearful of drawing too
close to decoration, which was the reason he would reach
for spatial or artistic justifications for anything he created
that might seem contrary to his earlier rhetoric. This was
not necessarily the way contemporaries viewed his work,
however. When the Swiss Pavilion opened in 1933, for
example, the critic for *Beaux-Arts* saw the arrangement of
colors on the walls as "the true ornament" of the building,

181
182

with "each surface being adorned with a single color, but two colors, sometimes related, sometimes contrasting violently, often sharing nearby adjacent surfaces, which intersect or are face-to-face with one another. One cannot deny that these 'divided' combinations have a very attractive decorative value."[5]

At the same time, figurative and ornamental elements began to appear in his buildings. This was inadvertent, he explained, in the case of the photographic mural in the Swiss Pavilion (see fig. 146). From his many versions of the circumstances that gave rise to this mural, it seems that the administration demanded "under dire threats" that he cover a curved masonry wall in the library with a mural of "large pictures representing rocks, clouds, and glaciers etc., etc., . . . recalling their native land to the poor incoming students lost in dangerous Paris."[6] He "thought up the idea of a 'photo-mural.' He had collected a mass of material . . . supplemented by views of microbiology and micro-mineralogy. These were blown up at frantic speed and stuck on the wall,"[7] forming a gridlike composition of greatly enlarged photographs that covered its entire surface, a graphic device he had already used in *L'Esprit Nouveau*.[8] Similar photographs were applied to a column in the adjacent entry hall (fig. 182). The subjects covered a wide range, from microcellular images of organic and geologic nature to aerial landscape views and stacks of manmade objects, but pattern and surface were emphasized, with the contrasting dark and light squares creating a dynamic checkerboard effect.[9] For Le Corbusier, a mural made of modern, blown-up, mostly abstract images laid out as a grid and mechanically produced as a photomontage was a monument to a new communication technology and would not challenge his strictures against traditional decoration. "By its very intensity, this mural was," in Charlotte Perriand's assessment, "an act of faith, an architectural assertion." But curiously, on a decorative level, she tells us, "it was completed by a large table that occupied a precise position, fastened to the floor by two lacquered steel tubes fitted with a pair of cast-iron disks and supporting a very heavy slab of white marble, carefully selected for its veining."[10]

Other flirtations with decorative embellishment were not so inadvertent, and could not so easily be excused by rhetoric or circumstance. In 1931, when Le Corbusier teamed up with Salubra to produce his collection of wallpapers, he had justified the use of color as a spatial element, as he had done with the painted walls in his Purist houses: "I have made a selection [of colored papers] guided by only architectural preoccupations," he maintained, in order to create an architectural animation, not a decorative addition.

183 184

"I do not believe in *tapestry*," he added, "because with tapestry one can make indifferently Louis XIV, Turkish or Primavera [referring to the design boutique of Le Printemps department store], and lie at every hour of the day. I believe in a *wall* animated with one color. I project it in the architectural symphony with the same strength that confers on it *its dimensions* and *its proportions*, in geometry and color."[11] But just a few years later, he did an about face and designed a figurative tapestry as one of a group of artists including Dufy, Léger, Miró, and Picasso commissioned by the collector Marie Cuttoli to provide cartoons for weaving at the historic factories at Aubusson. After the war Le Corbusier was drawn much deeper into this medium at the request of Pierre Baudouin, a designer at Aubusson. Beginning in 1948 and continuing until his death, he sporadically designed tapestry cartoons in collaboration with Baudouin, still lifes (fig. 183) and figurative works (fig. 184) that followed the vivid imagery of his postwar painting, woven with flat areas in organic shapes and bright colors and overlaid with a fluid, descriptive line. He was able to defend this new devotion to a medium that he had so decidedly condemned by changing its intent, legitimizing tapestry by positioning it no longer as a "sort of picture framed by garlands . . . suspended in the middle of a wall," but as a latter-day mural painting, made for the "nomadic man that we have become. . . . Our nomad moves house

because his family has grown larger, or, on the contrary, because his children have married. The tapestry gives him the possibility of providing himself with a 'mural,' that is to say, a painting of large dimensions, of architectural potential. He unrolls his tapestry and spreads it on the wall, reaching to the floor. Does he want to move? He rolls up his 'mural,' puts it under his arm and goes downstairs to install it in its new location."[12]

Regardless of his sentiment about the nomadic nature of our possessions, Le Corbusier also painted murals, just before the war. What seems to have changed his earlier attitude toward the painted, and figurative, elaboration of the wall surface was Picasso's large and powerful, monochromatic *Guernica*, which he admired when it was first shown at the Exposition Internationale des Arts et Techniques dans la Vie Modern in Paris in 1937. In a journal notation of 1950 considering the idea for a book, *The Murals of Corbu*,[13] he totaled up fifteen that he had painted, seven on the walls of E. 1027, the house by the sea at Roquebrune that Eileen Gray had designed for Jean Badovici, publisher of *Architecture Vivante*. This controversial series, with sexual imagery painted both in vibrant color and in grisaille (fig. 185), has been seen as an act of vandalism on the part of Le Corbusier, who altered without Gray's permission her conception of the building as totally white and flat, a conception that had been developed very much under the

influence of Le Corbusier himself. While most of his fifteen murals were, like these, done privately, in 1948 he was asked to replace the photomural in the library at the Swiss Pavilion, which had been destroyed during the Nazi occupation of Paris, with another. Painting quickly, directly on the masonry wall, he executed a large mythological subject in vivid polychrome, which he complemented later, in 1957, with movable banquettes similarly polychromed, done in enamels (fig. 186).

More universal than his involvement in pictorial, symbolic decoration in the form of tapestry, mural painting, and enamel (a relatively minor moment in his career), but always secondary to his visionary volumes bathed in light, was his engagement in bringing pattern to the surface. This intention had been announced in his introduction to the first Salubra wallpaper series, where he christened each of his "architectural" hues "with a title descriptive of its significance in mural effect, such as 'space,' 'sky,' 'velvet,' 'sand.'"[14] Pattern too, deliberate and demonstrative, appears throughout his postwar works. Even in the early 1930s, when he created the first series of his Salubra wallpapers, he had included a collection of "seeded," or polka-dot, patterns (fig. 187), which he said "should be utilized with discretion; their purpose is to give life and interest to portions of surface which are not constantly in the direct line of vision, such as ceilings, niches, dadoes, and individual panels. . . .

186

The aim in producing these 'seeded' patterns is to provide something in the nature of a decorative accessory."[15] When the second wallpaper series was issued in 1959, he introduced even bolder patterns, marble designs in various colors (fig. 188), which were now more than decorative "accessories." These papers, which he described as "very powerful,"[16] could be hung in horizontal or vertical arrangements to become the dramatic focus of an entire wall. This was demonstrated in the interiors photographed for Salubra's advertisements (fig. 189), which showed the wallpaper as appropriate settings for "modern" furniture, both the firm's metal designs of 1928 and the work of others.

Along with his new emphasis on texture and pattern, the role of color had changed. The Purist palette that continued into the 1930s (and even later, although somewhat altered, in the second Salubra wallpaper series) gave way to an insistent use of primaries and secondaries, while the constructive employment of color to manipulate space, which he had described in his "Architectural Polychromy," yielded to festive pageantry and subjective expressionism, from the symphony of colors on the interior streets in Marseilles to the red and purple side chapels at Ronchamp. The flat colors with which he painted the balconies at Marseilles and the ceilings of the dormitory rooms in the Brazilian Pavilion in Paris (1958)—and repainted those at the Swiss Pavilion (redone in 1958)—created bold, elemental statements, like an Ellsworth Kelly painting, using color as a decorative, expressive medium.[17]

Although he positioned furniture as a subject for continued polemical discussion, as a practical matter by the 1950s he had given up on his own furniture design, frustrated that his clients had not offered him the opportunity to expand upon his ideas of how best to make objects reflect the realities of modern life. Le Corbusier had already yielded to Charlotte Perriand the details of furnishing the Marseilles block, and in general he seemed to have come to terms with what he could and could not do in this regard. "In the matter of furniture," Le Corbusier wrote in the *Oeuvre complète* in 1957, "it can be affirmed that the future is not sketched out. Everything depends upon truly stating the conditions of life of modern society, of architecture, and of domestic furnishings. . . . Here, in the Jaoul Houses at Neuilly," he noted simply, "the problem of furniture has not been dealt with."[18] This is unfortunate because for this house he had provided well-defined ideas for built-in storage, seating, and tables, which he presented in a series of colored drawings (fig. 190). He continued to design a considerable array of storage units to outfit his houses architecturally, but he was now resigned to accept whatever furniture his clients chose for their interiors.

But for Le Corbusier "an essential part of the solution" of the problems of furniture had already been achieved with the completion of his *unités d'habitation*, and his underlying social vision for them that projected living arrangements as temporary, based on changing family circumstances. His idea of nomad inhabitants moving up and down in the scale of their apartments in true Socialist fashion according to their needs altered the concept of possessions as well, since they too would need to be temporary, expanding and contracting with each move. "War, bombings," he wrote almost jubilantly, "have destroyed homes and furnishings; the new generations can set themselves

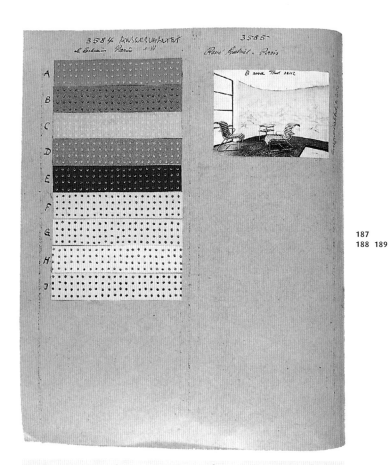

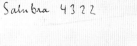

187
188 189

187 "Seeded" wallpaper pattern. From Salubra Collection (1931). **188** Marble wallpaper pattern. From Second Salubra Collection (1959).
189 Advertisement for Salubra wallpaper. From *Zodiac* (1960).

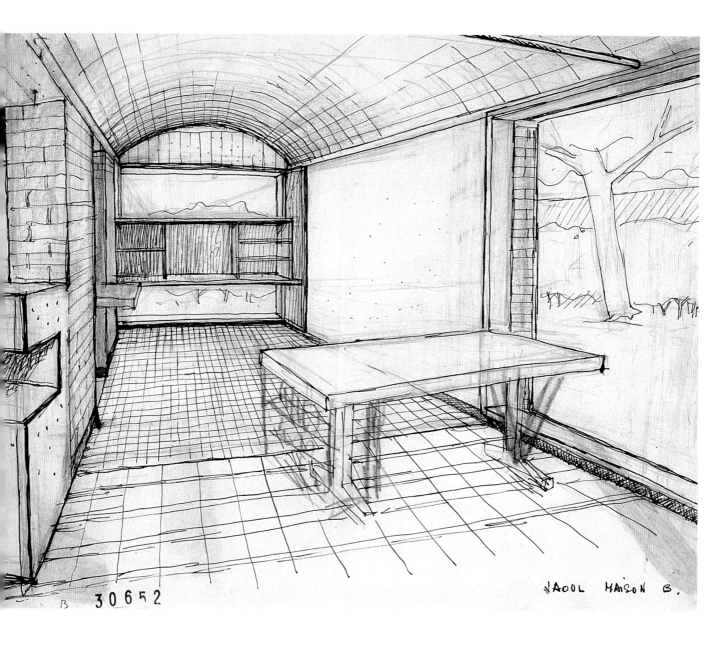

Raoul. Maison B   C 30652   30 oct 53

190

191

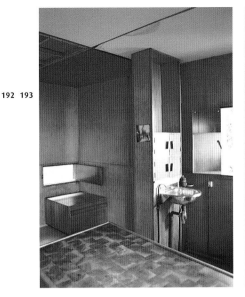 

192 193

up in housekeeping without bearing the burden of inherited 'family furniture.' Henceforth they shall be able to enter their apartment with their valises in hand, their bookcase, their bedding and their clothing. All that remains is to provide beds (and what simplified beds!) tables (and what concerns tables—size, combinations of possible juxtapositions?) and finally the seating (what concerns seating?)."[19]

Le Corbusier provided little other than these basics for the interior of the rustic cabin (*le cabanon*) he built for himself by the sea at Roquebrune in the South of France in 1950–52 (fig. 191). Here, too, he chose to announce symbolically the meaning of his cabin. Just as he had introduced metaphoric allusions in the photographs of his interiors and created a village street high up in his *unités,* he ultimately (after rejecting aluminum and then clapboard) wrapped this modern prefabricated cabin with rough, split logs, investing the little structure by the sea with the trappings and the associations of a remote forest retreat. The prefabricated cabin is as shipshape as any building he designed, a space less than 4 meters square created in accordance with the measurements of the Modulor, in which everything that would be needed was completely planned in advance (it had neither a kitchen, for it faced the terrace of a restaurant, nor a shower, for the sea was at hand). Its interior was clad with unpainted plywood panels and was furnished sparsely with built-in wooden bed, counters, and tables, and the most rudimentary of seating (figs. 192, 193). But it was not bereft of decorative effect; in addition to emphasizing the grain of its plywood walls, Le Corbusier elaborated a program of colored accents (figs. 194, 195), with painted cabinets, paintings treated as murals, and large panels of flat color painted on the ceiling above the bed. It was here that Le Corbusier came with his wife, Yvonne, to get away from it all, leaving his practice and possessions behind in Paris. Here he enjoyed a Spartan existence by the sea in this most minuscule of spaces, furnished with the most basic of chairs, tables, and storage. For the modern nomad that he wanted to be, anything else would have been an encumbrance.

NOTES

1. *Le Corbusier et Pierre Jeanneret: Oeuvre complète 1934–1938,* ed. Max Bill (Zurich: Editions Dr. H. Girsberger, 1939), 125.
2. Ibid.
3. *Le Corbusier et son atelier rue de Sèvres 35: Oeuvre complète 1952–1957,* ed. W. Boesiger, 2nd ed. (Zurich: Editions Girsberger, 1958), 115.
4. Sigfried Giedion, *Space, Time and Architecture: The Growth of a New Tradition,* 5th ed. (Cambridge, Mass.: Harvard University Press, 1967), liii, 546.
5. G. Brunon Guardia, "La Maison Suisse de la Cité Universitaire," *Beaux-Arts,* July 14, 1933, 1.
6. Quoted in Daniele Naegele, "Le Corbusier and the Space of Photography: Photo-Murals, Pavilions and Multi-Media Spectacles," *History of Photography,* Summer 1998, 131.
7. Le Corbusier, *Creation Is a Patient Search,* trans. James Palmes (New York: Frederick A. Praeger, 1960), 98.
8. See, for example, *L'Esprit Nouveau* 14 and 19 (1924).
9. The mural images and Le Corbusier's use of photography is discussed by Naegele, op. cit., 127–38.
10. Charlotte Perriand, *Une Vie de crèation* (Paris: Editions Odile Jacob, 1998), 53.
11. Le Corbusier, "Architectural Polychromy," in *Polychromie Achitecturale: Le Corbusier's Color Keyboards from 1931 and 1959,* ed. Arthur Rüegg (Basel, Boston,and Berlin: Birkhäuser Verlag, 1997), 141 [translation modified].
12. *Oeuvre complète 1952–1957,* 133.
13. *Le Corbusier Sketchbooks, 1950–1954* (New York: Architectural History Foundation; and Cambridge, Mass., and London: MIT Press, 1981), 22.
14. Le Corbusier, "Colour Keyboards," reproduced in *Polychromie Architecturale.*
15. Ibid.
16. "Second Salubra Collection by Le Corbusier," reproduced in *Polychromie Architecturale.*
17. Kelly had in fact visited the *unité d'habitation* in Marseilles in 1952 and found the colored *brises-soleil* of the balconies a revelation. "The wide slabs in primary colors . . . surprised me," he recollected in 1991, "but I thought that Le Corbusier was using color in a decorative way. I wanted to use color in this way, over an entire wall, but I didn't want it to be decorative"; quoted in Yve-Alain Bois, Jack Cowart, and Alfred Pacquement, *Ellsworth Kelly: The Years in France, 1948–1954* (Washington, D.C.: National Gallery of Art, 1992), 192.
18. *Oeuvre complète 1952–1957,* 208.
19. Ibid.

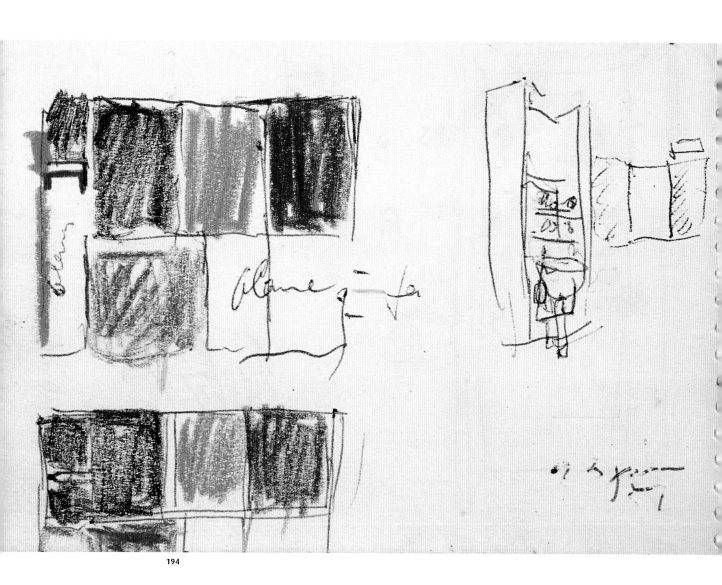

194

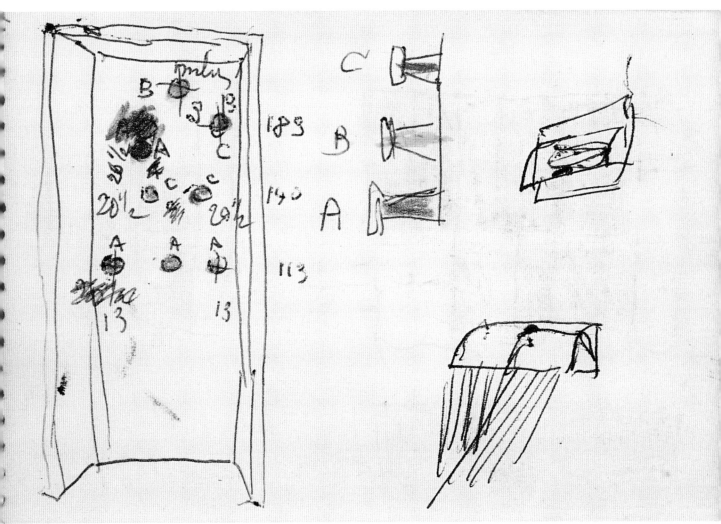

195

SELECTED BIBLIOGRAPHY

Baker, Geoffrey H. *Le Corbusier—The Creative Search: The Formative Years of Charles-Edouard Jeanneret*. New York: Von Nostrand Reinhold, 1996.

Benton, Tim. *The Villas of Le Corbusier, 1920-1930*. New Haven and London: Yale University Press, 1987.

Brooks, H. Allen. *Le Corbusier's Formative Years: Charles Edouard Jeanneret at La Chaux-de-Fonds*. Chicago and London: University of Chicago Press, 1997.

De Fusco, Renato. *Le Corbusier, Designer: Furniture, 1929*. Woodbury, N.Y.: Barrons, 1977.

Di Puolo, Maurizio, Marcello Fagiolo, and Maria Luisa Madonna, eds. *Le Corbusier, Charlotte Perriand, Pierre Jeanneret: "La machine à s'asseoir."* Rome: De Luca Editore, 1976.

L'Esprit Nouveau: Le Corbusier et l'industrie 1920-1925. Strasbourg: Les Musées de Ville de Strasbourg, 1987.

L'Esprit Nouveau: Revue Internationale Illustrée de Ol'Activité Contemporaine. 28 nos., 1920-25. Reprint, New York: Da Capo Press, 1968.

Gans, Deborah. *The Le Corbusier Guide*. Rev. ed. New York: Princeton Architectural Press, 2000.

Le Corbusier. *Almanach d'architecture moderne*. Paris: Les Editions G. Crès et Cie, 1926.

——. *Creation Is a Patient Search*. James Palmes, trans. New York, Frederick A. Praeger Publishers, 1960.

——. *The Decorative Art of Today*. James I. Dunnett, trans. Cambridge, Mass.: MIT Press, 1987.

——. *Modulor I and II*. Peter de Francia and Anna Bostock, trans. Cambridge, Mass.: Harvard University Press, 1980.

——. *Precisions on the Present State of Architecture and City Planning . . . .* Edith Schreiber Aujame, trans. Cambridge, Mass., and London: MIT Press, 1991.

——. *The Radiant City: Elements of a Doctrine of Urbanism To Be Used as the Basis of Our Machine-Age Civilization*. New York: Orion Press, 1967.

——. *Towards a New Architecture*. Frederick Etchells, trans. London: John Rodker Publisher, 1927.

——. *Voyage d'Orient: Carnets*. New York: Rizzoli, 1988.

Le Corbusier, et al. *Oeuvre complète*. 7 vols. Zurich: Editions d'Architecture, 1973-77.

The Le Corbusier Archives. H. Allen Brooks, ed. 32 vols. New York: Garland Publishing, and Paris: Fondation Le Corbusier, 1982-84.

Le Corbusier: Painter and Architect. Fonden til Udgivelse af Arkitekturtidsskrift B, 1995.

Le Corbusier Sketchbooks. 4 vols. New York: Architectural History Foundation, and Cambridge, Mass.: MIT Press, 1981-82.

Le Corbusier: Une encyclopédie. Paris: Centre Georges Pompidou, 1987.

Lyon, Dominique, et al. *Le Corbusier Alive*. Paris: Vilo International, 2000.

Mathias, Martine. *Le Corbusier: Oeuvre tissé*. Paris: Philippe Sers, 1987.

Perriand, Charlotte. *Une Vie de création*. Paris: Editions Odile Jacob, 1998.

Rüegg, Arthur, ed. *Polychromie Architecturale: Le Corbusier's Color Keyboards from 1931 and 1959*. Basel, Boston, and Berlin: Birkhäuser, 1997.

ACKNOWLEDGMENTS

Researching the architecture and design of Le Corbusier and his associates enjoys an advantage over that of most other recent figures: an archive and a library that set the standard for accessibility. The Fondation Le Corbusier, established by the bequest of Le Corbusier and now headed by Evelyne Tréhin, includes hundreds of thousands of documents of the master and his firm and over thirty thousand original drawings. The drawings have all been published in a series of large-format volumes, while the documents can be accessed by computer and viewed onscreen at the Fondation's headquarters in the Villa Jeanneret in Paris. The Fondation's determination to welcome all serious research on Le Corbusier's work makes it a pleasure to use these resources, and the director and staff could not be more helpful in their commitment to furthering this goal.

While archival research was at the core of my thinking, individual insights have brought me a different kind of understanding of the architect's work. Richard Bisch generously took time out to share his experiences at and his strong feelings about Le Corbusier's Marseilles project, where he has lived for almost half a century. He also made available his photographs of the building taken over many decades. On a different level, Ralph Lieberman, an architectural historian, a talented photographer, and a valued friend, opened my eyes to dimensional aspects of Le Corbusier's architecture when I was focusing more narrowly on design issues. His photographs of the Villa Savoye and the Villa Jeanneret have helped this book to come startlingly alive. Jacqueline Robin, administrator of the Villa Savoye, graciously made this extraordinary monument of twentieth-century architecture fully accessible for photography. Others who have been helpful in putting this book together include Rachel Brishoual, Isabella Colombo, Sonia Eduard, Philippe Garner, Kathryn B. Hiesinger, Elizabeth Höier, Danielle Ianton, Lilah Mittelstaedt, Andreas Nutz, Lynn Rosenthal, and Mark Tucker.

The early encouragement of Gianfranco Monacelli and Andrea Monfried allowed me to revisit a subject that I had investigated somewhat less intensively earlier, while Ron Broadhurst's counsel about the importance of context helped me to bring more fully into focus the significance of Le Corbusier's furniture and interiors. Finally, Tracey Shiffman and Annabelle Gould gave this book a design that is not just incredibly smart but intelligent as well.

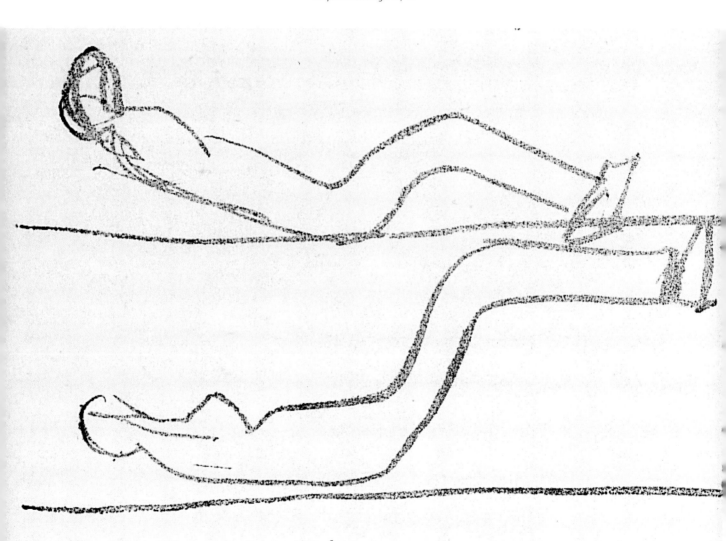